Llyn Cerrig Bach is a small lake, rippled by the wind and surrounded by reeds. It is not well known, even on the Isle of Anglesey. However Llyn Cerrig Bach is an extraordinary place because of its ancient history. The Iron Age artefacts uncovered there continue to fascinate archaeologists, and the story of their discovery still captures the public imagination.

LLYN CERRIG BACH
Treasure from the Iron Age

Compiled and produced for Oriel Ynys Môn
by Llyfrau Magma, Llansadwrn, Ynys Môn LL59 5SR

Writer and editor

Philip Steele

Archaeological consultant

Frances Lynch

Contributors

Miranda Aldhouse-Green
Peter and Susan Crew
Andrew Davidson
Mary Davis
Adam Gwilt
Frances Lynch
Philip Macdonald
Meirion MacIntyre Huws
Evelyn Owen-Jones
George Smith
Tim Young

Project management & design

Robert Williams

© *Llyfrau Magma and contributors* 2012

Ar gael hefyd yn yr iaith Gymraeg:
Llyn Cerrig Bach: Trysor o'r Oes Haearn
ISBN 978–1–902565–12–5

Oriel Ynys Môn
**Rhosmeirch, Llangefni
Ynys Môn LL77 7TQ Wales**

CYNGOR SIR
YNYS MÔN
ISLE OF ANGLESEY
COUNTY COUNCIL

ISBN 978–1–902565–14–9

Foreword

The wartime discovery, in 1942/43, of an astonishingly well-preserved collection of artefacts, once cast into an ancient lake at Llyn Cerrig Bach, had tremendous impact on our understanding of the Iron Age in Britain. It remains a particular high point in the collecting history of Amgueddfa Cymru — National Museum Wales. This remarkable story owes a special debt to Sir Cyril Fox, previous Director (1926-1948) and leading archaeologist. His wartime efforts, together with the invaluable help of airfield staff making and reporting the discovery, were instrumental in securing and keeping together this exceptional discovery for the nation. His research and original report generated pivotal new understanding of religious practice, Celtic art and chariot design, and did much to promote the international importance of this site.

Today, the National Museum continues to be a centre of research and learning across Wales. Museum professionals unlock, present and share new stories about collections, working hard to make them accessible to the diverse interests and needs of its many users and visitors. Each year, it also offers support to regional museums, keen to borrow and exhibit national collections in new and innovative ways. I am convinced that, wherever possible, the National Museum should respond generously, always aware that cultural treasures hold particular meanings and connections for people living across Wales.

I warmly welcome this engaging book, commissioned by Oriel Ynys Môn, to coincide with an exhibition of treasures from Llyn Cerrig Bach on Anglesey. Within its covers, we are offered the rich insights of archaeologists, researchers, passionate supporters and the author, showing how archaeological understanding is constantly generated, growing and changing. Llyn Cerrig Bach never ceases to offer intriguing insights into our identities, past and present.

David Anderson
Director General, Amgueddfa Cymru
— National Museum Wales 2012

ORIEL YNYS MÔN, the Isle of Anglesey's principal museum and gallery, is located ten miles from one of the most important archaeological sites in Wales — Llyn Cerrig Bach. It is generally agreed that the treasure found in the lake represents offerings to the Celtic gods, cast into the waters more than two thousand years ago.

The Oriel is proud to spotlight this remarkable example of the island's rich heritage with this book: the first accessible account ever to be published.

It includes many new insights contributed by archaeologists and other specialists on the treasure and its significance.

Pat West
Oriel Ynys Môn
Isle of Anglesey County Council

ANGLESEY

★ LLYN CERRIG BACH

A Lake in the West

The Isle of Anglesey forms the northernmost part of Wales, separated from the mainland by the Menai Strait. It has a mild and moist climate, typical of the western British Isles.

Anglesey's complex geological history is reflected in its coastline, which varies from broad estuaries and long beaches to sheer cliffs.

In the west, Holy Island forms an island in its own right, separated by a narrow tidal channel called Afon Lasinwen. This leads south from Four Mile Bridge to Cymyran Bay. The coast southwards is dominated in many places by extensive sand dunes, stabilised by clumps of stiff marram grass and bordered by farmland.

Llyn Cerrig Bach (OS114 SH306765) is located 1·5 kilometres (one mile) inland, near the village of Llanfair yn Neubwll. Cerrig Bach means 'small stones' in Welsh, but the name Llyn Cerrig Bach does not derive from a description of the lake shore. It was named after a nearby smallholding, Cerrig Bach, which lay to the east of the lake.

The landscape here is mostly fen with reedbeds and scrub, broken by outcrops of rock. Small pools have formed where peat has been excavated in the past. Llyn Cerrig Bach is just one of a number of small lakes, including Penrhyn, Dinam, Treflesg and the Traffwll reservoir. These are visited by waterfowl and warblers, and the area is designated both as a Site of Special Scientific Interest and as a Reserve of the RSPB.

Such is the environment seen today by local farmers, by naturalists, by pilots and workers at the RAF base, and by tourists visiting the small seaside town of Rhosneigr to the south. Has the land changed much since the Iron Age? The coastal dunes of western Anglesey have certainly been shifted and shaped by wind and waves over the ages, and one study has raised the possibility that the coastline itself may have moved westwards. However the Llyn Cerrig Bach artefacts show no trace of contact with saltwater, which does suggest that this was already a freshwater wetland environment in the Iron Age.

The greatest changes to this landscape since the Iron Age have been man-made, carried out during the nineteenth and twentieth centuries. In 1848 Robert Stephenson constructed the railway between Llanfair Pwllgwyngyll and Holyhead, the chief port for Ireland. The track passed immediately to the northwest of Llyn Cerrig Bach. Drainage for this engineering work is believed to have caused the silting up of much of the lake: indeed, people who lived here before the Second World War do not remember the lake as a notable landscape feature.

However even then the shape of the ancient lake would have been more apparent than it is today. The construction of the RAF Valley airfield in the 1940s had a drastic impact and utterly changed the area of the lake and its surrounds. It was this intrusion which led to the discovery of the treasure, some two thousand years after it had been left there.

A small lake on the Isle of Anglesey has an ancient secret that it has kept for over two thousand Years ...

F 1099b

Railway

Llyn
Cerrig
Bach

Llyn Dinam

N

(**this page**) *The area of peat-spreading at
RAF Valley in the Second World War is marked
on a reconnaissance photograph of the runways,
taken at the time by the German Luftwaffe.
The dredging site is located by the star.*

(**opposite page**) *A 'Flying Fortress' of the
United States Army Air Forces.*

1 A WARTIME DISCOVERY

THE ROYAL AIR FORCE opened its airfield near Llyn Cerrig Bach during the Second World War, on 13th February 1941. The station was briefly called RAF Rhosneigr, before being renamed RAF Valley.

Anglesey's strategic importance derived from its proximity to the great port of Liverpool, 100 kilometres (60 miles) to the east. Liverpool's docks were vital to the war effort and convoys of merchant ships left from there on the trans-Atlantic crossing to North America, stalked by German U-boats. In the Battle of the Atlantic as a whole, Allied fatalities included 36,200 naval personnel and 36,000 merchant sea-men. Enemy fatalities numbered about 30,000.

German bombers stationed in Occupied France made their approach to Liverpool over the Irish Sea. About half of the homes in central Liverpool were damaged by German bombing during the war, resulting in the deaths of some 2,500 people. The glow from the Liverpool 'blitz' could be seen on the horizon from Anglesey's east coast.

Inevitably RAF Valley was soon playing a very important part in the war. Its aircraft were used for patrolling the Irish Sea, for attacking enemy aircraft, for protecting convoys and for rescue. Many foreign airmen were stationed here, including at times Czechs, Poles, Australians and Belgians. At the height of operations, service personnel numbered about 500 men and women.

Ironically, aerial reconnaissance photographs taken by the *Luftwaffe* at this time have since assisted archaeologists in establishing the progress of engineering work on the runways around Llyn Cerrig Bach.

In 1942 the runways had to be extended to accommodate large American bombers such as the Boeing B-17 'Flying Fortress'. USAAF pilots arrived in 1943, when Valley became a terminal for receiving new aeroplanes from the USA and Canada, which were then delivered to other British airfields. After Victory in Europe, the base was used in the transfer of aircraft from the European theatre of war to the Far East.

The Valley runways were constructed across the common land of Tywyn Trewan, a tract of sand and gorse beside Afon Crigyll. This bleak landscape had been made famous in the popular Welsh-language historical novel *Madam Wen* (written by W.D. Owen of Rhosneigr in the 1920s).

It was said that the airmen at this time had a second enemy with which to contend, namely the never-ending windblown sand. Along the beaches of Anglesey's west coast, the full force of a gale has always been formidable, whipping up grains of sand in stinging fusillades. In this case the laying of the runways had removed the vegetation that bound the sand, and sowing with grass had failed to stabilise the soil. Sand was now getting everywhere and, most seriously, it was penetrating the aircraft engines. It was decided that the easiest way to solve this problem was by covering the sand alongside the runways with peat from the adjacent wetlands.

A WORLD WAR THROWS UP EVIDENCE OF BATTLES AND CONFLICTS IN A MORE DISTANT AGE

OUT OF THE PEAT

Peat was being extracted from the wetlands around RAF Valley from October 1942. This work had a major impact on the natural environment, through excavation, flooding and the infilling of peaty areas with sand removed from the airfield. The rich black soil was removed by a steel scoop which travelled on a wire, reeled by two cable engines – a kind of dragline. The scoop dumped the peat on the rock beside the lake, and left it to drain. It was then shifted on to lorries and taken to the runway construction sites. Here it was spread by tractors with harrows.

One day a harrow caught on an iron chain. The chain was freed and removed, only to be commandeered for use as a makeshift tow rope. The chain was used to haul lorries which had become bogged down in the mud. The linkage was strong and performed well. The head groundsman supervising the work, W.O. Roberts, noted the unusual design and apparent age of the chain, and took it to J.A. Jones, the resident engineer, whose job was to direct the construction of the runway extensions.

The ground staff recalled that other items, such as an iron tyre, had been turned up during excavation, and flung back in the bog as scrap. The workers soon developed a keen interest in keeping their eyes open for other pieces of metalwork. On 8 July 1943 J.A. Jones wrote to the National Museum of Wales in Cardiff, sending drawings of several items that had been recovered. Their importance was immediately recognised and the tractor chain was confirmed as being a gang chain for slaves, dating back to the Late Iron Age.

With official backing, more items were now sought. All items found, of any period, were to be kept for examination. Many were turned up by W.O. Roberts and by fellow workers R. Roberts, W. Jones and W. Rees.

(right) A selection of items from the treasure, impressive in their variety.
(below) A plan for the London & North West Railway track (1929/1930) shows that water was drawn from nearby lakes to supply steam locomotives. This may also have changed water levels in the area between the 1840s and the 1940s.

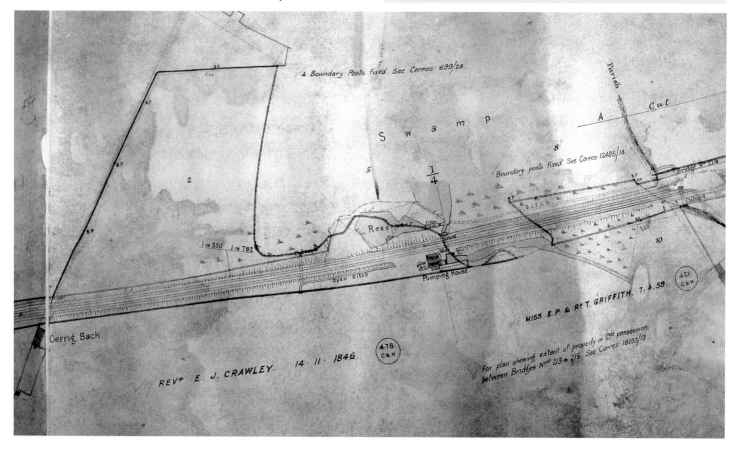

ANY OLD IRON — OR AN UNEXPECTED HAUL OF TREASURE?

A remarkable find at Valley

How did an Iron Age slave chain come to be used to haul lorries?
Evelyn Owen-Jones remembers her father's role in the discovery of the treasure

At the start of the Second World War in 1939, my father William Owen Roberts of Llanfaelog was keeper of the greens at the Anglesey Golf Club in Rhosneigr, so he had plenty of experience in dealing with the problems of turf and windblown sand.

These skills were put to the test when a new RAF station came to be constructed at Valley. Due to my father's knowledge of the local terrain, he was employed by the Ministry of War Transport as Head Groundsman at the airfield, which lies adjacent to the golfing greens.

When the USA entered the war, Valley became a staging post in the trans-Atlantic deployment of Flying Fortresses and Liberators. These large bombers needed long extensions to the runways in order to be able to land safely. The engineering work had many implications for local people. For example, the family of Evan Hughes, living at the smallholding of Cae Ifan near Llyn Cerrig Bach, now perilously near the runways, had to be moved to a more secure location in the village of Caergeiliog.

For my father and his work team at Valley, the job was to find a way of stabilising the sandy soil, which had been levelled, stripped of natural windbreaks and its marram grass. The solution suggested by my father was to dredge peat from the local bogs and to spread it over the runway margins.

From the autumn of 1942 the buckets hauled the peat to the banks and the workers shovelled it onto lorries bound for those sites designated for runway extension. One day a lorry became stuck in thick mud, and needed a tow from the tractor. Unfortunately the wire tow rope broke, and a replacement had to be found. This also parted, so my father went to retrieve an old chain which he had previously noticed lying in the mud. He fitted it to the tractor. This chain linkage saw repeated service that day and stood up to the stress and strain without difficulty.

At the end of a hard day's work, my father looked more carefully at the unusual construction of this chain. He draped it over the handlebars of his bicycle and trudged off to see the resident engineer, Mr J.A.Jones, whose office was at the Rhosneigr end of the airfield. It was a walk of over a mile – and one with momentous consequences.

When a sketch of the improvised tow rope was sent to the National Museum of Wales in Cardiff, it was identified as a gang chain for slaves or captives, perhaps 2,000 years old. My father and the work team found further pieces of iron and bronze in the months and years that followed. My father sent some of these off to Cardiff himself, postage one shilling, and I still have letters of thanks to him from the museum's director, Sir Cyril Fox.

To this day my father's role in dredging the peat, in drawing attention to the iron chain and making many further discoveries, remains a matter of great pride to me and my family.

The story of the Llyn Cerrig Bach treasure continues to inspire the youngsters I talk to at Anglesey's primary schools – I am a former teacher – and it arouses interest worldwide.

Evelyn Owen-Jones lectures to schools, historical and archaeological societies, and community groups

AMGUEDDFA GENEDLAETHOL CYMRU

VICE-PRESIDENT : SIR LEONARD TWISTON DAVIES, K.B.E., F.S.A.   TREASURER : DAVID E. ROBERTS, ESQ:, M.Inst
DIRECTOR : SIR CYRIL FOX, P.S.A., F.B.A.

TELEPHONE 5873   F/MD

NATIONAL MUSEUM OF WALES
CARDIFF

25th June, 1947.

Dear Mr.Roberts,

I am glad you **like** the Book, and
am pleased to know that you are still head groundsman and
will continue to look out, with the men under you, for
Llyn Cerrig things on the airfield.

Please send along the bits of iron
you speak of as soon as possible.   We shall be pleased to
have them.

Yours sincerely,

W.O.Roberts Esq.,
5, Rehoboth Terrace,
Llanfaelog,
Ty Croes,
Anglesey.

Director.

(above) W.O.Roberts despatched finds from the airfield to Sir Cyril Fox.
(below) A gang chain is used to demonstrate its function, shackling slaves by the neck.

"The make-up of the collection is predominantly masculine, a bracelet being probably the only thing which might have belonged to a woman; it is moreover overwhelmingly military in character. More than half the finds are metal fittings from chariot or pony-harness; and the numerous swords and spears—which are the two weapons shown by continental burials to be carried by the warrior in his chariot—are consistent with the probability that the deposit, in its military aspect, is solely concerned with this form of warfare. Viewed in another aspect, it is an exceptionally varied group-find, since it consists of over thirty categories of objects."

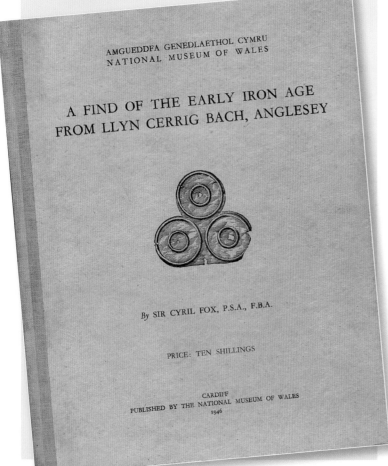

CALLING IN THE EXPERTS

In August 1943 Sir Cyril Fox, director of the National Museum of Wales in Cardiff, arrived at Valley. He talked with the workforce and engineers. He established that all the artefacts seemed to have come from the same part of the wetlands, evidence pointing to a strip of bog named Cors yr Ynys, which had been excavated to a depth of about 3½ metres. The bog had flanked the southwestern shore of silted up Llyn Cerrig Bach, but the recent dredging had already returned this area to the waters of the lake.

Cyril Fox was particularly interested in a platform of rock at the edge of an outcrop, known as Craig Carnau'r Ebolion ('Rock of the Colts' Hooves' would be one possible translation), or just Craig y Carnau. This outcrop took its name from a local farm; it would become known to the RAF by a more technical term – TACAN (Tactical Air Navigation) hill. Fox surmised that this rocky platform could have been the original point from which the metal objects were thrown into the lake as votive offerings.

He searched in vain for traces of ancient settlement around the rock and the smallholding of Cae Ifan. However he did not rule out the possibility that people had lived on the lakeshore in the Iron Age, pointing out that since time immemorial farmers have carted off ancient stones and re-used them for walls and buildings.

Fox returned to the site twice in 1944 and again in 1945. Legal ownership of the assemblage was resolved and the items were dispatched to the National Museum in Cardiff, for cataloguing, conservation and research.

Fox speculated that further treasure existed, but feared that it must have been scattered under the runways of this busy airfield, or buried by subsequent building work. By the end of the Second World War part of Llyn Cerrig Bach had been filled in to support the airfield's perimeter road. The site had changed entirely, including both the area occupied by the lake and its depth.

Fox's final report was completed in 1946, and published in May 1947 by the National Museum of Wales. The assemblage was illustrated in fine detail by C.O. Waterhouse. The book was a masterpiece of analysis and discussion, which is still admired by archaeologists today. It raised the big questions – when, why and where? Fox's estimate of the date of the assemblage was approximately from the second century BC to the Roman conquest, a period of time which, as we shall see, has since been revised.

Fox's findings have of course been refined, reinterpreted or challenged in the intervening years, notably his views on the geographical origins of some of the artefacts. Important publications dealing with Llyn Cerrig Bach have included *Prehistoric Anglesey* by Frances Lynch (second edition 1991) and *Llyn Cerrig Bach: A Study of the Copper Alloy Artefacts from the Insular La Tène Assemblage* by Philip Macdonald (2007).

Cyril Fox (right) carries out excavations at Ysceifiog, Flintshire, in 1927

Cyril Fox

At the time of the Llyn Cerrig Bach discovery Sir Cyril Fox (1882-1967) had been Director of the National Museum of Wales for seventeen years. He had been knighted in 1935 and was one of the leading archaeologists in Britain.

Born in Chippenham, he had been heading for a career in market gardening when he was given a job in Cambridge which led to an involvement with soils and archaeology, to a PhD in 1921, a post as Keeper of Archaeology in the National Museum of Wales in 1923 and as Director, in succession to Mortimer Wheeler, in 1926.

As an archaeologist he was essentially a historical geographer. His first book, *The Archaeology of the Cambridge Region* (1923) looked at the distribution through time of evidence for human settlement. This environmental approach informed perhaps his most influential book, *The Personality of Britain* (1932 with four editions to 1943 and a reprint in 1959), written when this lowlander had come to appreciate the crucial differences of highland Wales. Although primarily a prehistorian, while at the National Museum he studied the topography of the Early Mediaeval Offa's Dyke and the architecture of Monmouthshire houses, as well as the Early Bronze Age barrows of the Vale of Glamorgan before they fell under the tarmac of wartime airfields.

His work on the Iron Age finds from Llyn Cerrig Bach brought him a rich new area of research. After completing the detailed analysis of the finds in 1946 he broadened his approach to write a major work on the art of the Iron Age – *Pattern and Purpose; A survey of Early Celtic Art in Britain* published in 1958, ten years after his retirement from the museum. The finds from Anglesey are central to this book, and to all subsequent discussions of this art.   *Frances Lynch*

CYRIL FOX IMMEDIATELY RECOGNISED THE IMPORTANCE OF LLYN CERRIG BACH AND SET ABOUT THE CATALOGUING AND CONSERVATION OF ITS TREASURE

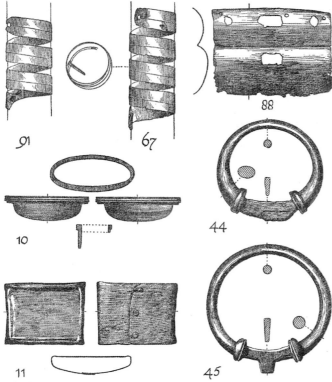

PLATE XV.—SCABBARD 8, DAGGER POMMEL 12, INNER RING OF NAVE-HOOP 39, CHARIOT-HORN CAP 41, LINCH-PIN 42, LOOPED FITTING 89.
References : 8, pp. 5, 73; 12, pp. 6, 74; 39, pp. 13, 76; 41, pp. 15, 19, 77; 42, pp. 19, 78; 89, pp. 58, 90.   Scale ⅜.

PLATE XVI.—SCABBARD MOUTH 10, SCABBARD BINDING 11, TERRETS 44, 45, BRONZE RIBBONS 67, 91, BRONZE PLATE 88.
References : 10, 11, pp. 6, 73, 74 ; 44, 45, pp. 35, 36, 79; 67, 91, pp. 45, 86, 90 ; 88, pp. 58, 90.   Scale ⅜.

THE TREASURE

Seen together in their original state, the finds at Llyn Cerrig Bach would have appeared as a jumble of ancient animal bones, a pile of old iron and pieces of bronze. The estimate of the total number of objects recovered depends to some extent on one's interpretation of the fragments: whether they are to be considered parts of complete artefacts or as separate items. Philip Macdonald in *Llyn Cerrig Bach* (2007) calculates the total number of items as 180, but dismisses ten of these as either modern depositions or as not dated with certainty to the Iron Age.

Some of the finds are magnificent and complete. Others are broken and partial, a jigsaw of pieces which have to be placed in position by archaeologists if the shapes of the original objects are to become apparent.

There are fragments of cauldrons, a crescent-shaped decorative plaque and also strips and squares of bronze. There are parts of war chariots or carts, and bridle bits for horses. There are swords, spears and a magnificent shield-boss. There are the remains of a large, curved horn. There are iron bars, probably used when trading in metals. There is a sickle, and two sets of iron tongs. There are two heavy iron chains, used to shackle captives or slaves. Iron and bronze objects may not be everybody's idea of treasure when compared with gold, silver or jewels, but these artefacts are certainly impressive. They are high status goods associated with wealth, religion, warfare and power.

It is arguable that some of the metalwork could have been hidden away in this remote spot, perhaps by a blacksmith for safekeeping in times of trouble. It has also been suggested that the treasure could be a cargo from an Iron Age shipwreck. However the most widely accepted theory is that most of the artefacts found at Llyn Cerrig Bach were ritual offerings made to the gods. Committing weapons, precious possessions or the booty of war to watery places as votive offerings was a common practice in Iron Age Britain and continental Europe.

Many of the objects had been deliberately spoiled or damaged in ancient times, perhaps to neutralise their 'power'. The bones (of oxen, horses, sheep or goats) showed no sign of having been butchered for meat, so were probably sacrificial remains.

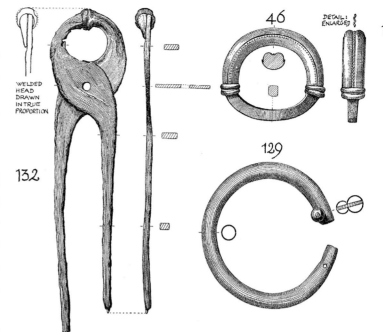

Current estimates suggest that items were left at the lake from the fourth or third century BC to perhaps the early second century AD. Because of this long timescale of deposition, archaeologists often refer to the finds as an 'assemblage' rather than as a one-off 'hoard'.

These are more than mere objects. They are a portal to another age. They tell us about people's lives, beliefs, hopes and fears over two thousand years ago. They remain one of the most important archaeological discoveries in Wales and provide valuable information about Iron Age Europe as a whole. In this book we shall be looking at the world which produced these artefacts, about the reasons why they may have been left at this site, about how they were discovered, conserved and researched.

The drawings by C.O. Waterhouse on these two pages include harness parts, chariot remains, bronze coils, metalworking tools and a spear head

PLATE XXIX.—GRIPPING-TONGS 132, HARNESS LOOP 46, BRIDLE-BIT RING 129.
References : 132, pp. 41, 96 ; 46, pp. 37, 79 ; 129, pp. 28, 95. Scale ⅔, except 46—½.

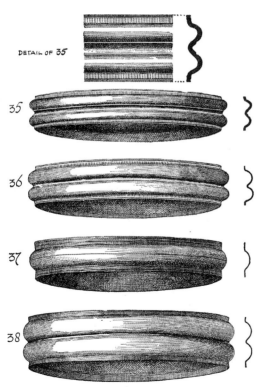

PLATE XVIII.—NAVE-HOOPS 35, 36, 37, 38.
References : pp. 13, 76. Scale ⅔ ; detail of 35, 4/3.

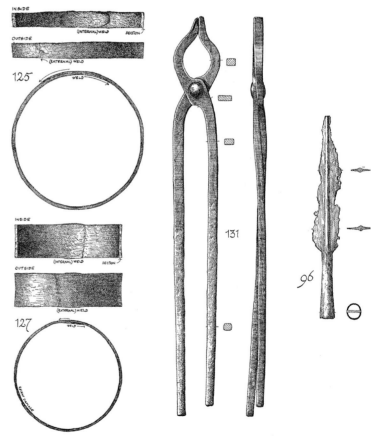

PLATE XIX.—NAVE-HOOPS 125, 126, TONGS 131, SPEAR 96.
References : 125, 127, pp. 15, 95 ; 131, pp. 41, 96 ; 96, pp. 6, 91. Scale ⅔, except 125—a little larger.

WEAPONS OF WAR AND THE TRAPPINGS OF WORLDLY POWER, OFFERED UP TO THE GODS ...

Conservation & technical research

How was the Llyn Cerrig Bach metalwork examined and saved for posterity?
Mary Davis *finds the methods of the 1940s and 50s very different from modern procedures*

Conservation was still quite a young science when the Llyn Cerrig Bach material was discovered, and there is relatively little documentary evidence concerning the early treatment of the assemblage.

However, from Sir Cyril Fox's account of the site and objects, it can be deduced that the burial conditions were stable and generally helpful to the survival of the objects. Many were preserved in relatively good condition. A striking example is the condition of the chains used to tow lorries out of the mud: Fox describes their condition when found as "probably perfect".

Peat is excellent for the preservation of many archaeological materials, as it is saturated, stagnant and contains little oxygen – the principal agent of decay. However, during the preparation of the airfield, the peat had been churned up and allowed to dry before being transported to the airfield sites, where it was spread onto sand and exposed for several months. Fox states how "Neither bronze nor iron objects suffered much from oxidation in the bog, but those of iron rusted considerably during the time they lay on the site".

After its discovery, much of the collection was sent to the British Museum for conservation. Fox states that "A great debt is owed to Dr. Plenderleith, whose skilled work reveals details not previously visible, and whose knowledge of craft techniques was placed unreservedly at the writer's disposal". Fox quotes extensively from Harold Plenderleith's notes, giving us some indication of the treatment some of the objects received.

An original description of the conservation of the horn survives. "The metal as received was in two pieces, badly crushed and under considerable strain. When folded back into shape after annealing [heat treatment], few of the badly corroded rivets had survived. The fractured ends of the metal were tacked together in position with soft solder, but it was clearly impossible to make a straight tube of it".

A relatively recent X-ray of the horn shows details of the rivets and the modern solder. These days objects such as this would not be re-straightened; annealing involves heating the metal to a relatively high temperature in order to change its internal structure. This makes the metal more malleable so it can be re-worked with less danger of cracking or breaking. Although annealing allows re-shaping, it also destroys potential evidence of the original crystal structure within the object, which could give information about ancient metalworking practices.

In 1991 a survey of all the iron work was undertaken in Cardiff, due to concern about the condition of the material. The report states that some of the artefacts revealed fresh corrosion and decaying lacquer; and early records show that some of the

(right) X-rays reveal a pelta mark on a sword blade.
(below) The Llyn Cerrig Bach horn – as found, x-rayed and restored.

objects had previously been electro-chemically stripped. Much of the iron was re-conserved, and then stored in desiccated conditions to help stabilise the iron.

X-radiography is an aspect of conservation routinely used for metals. X-rays of iron can be used to identify the form and shape of an object, and the extent of corrosion. X-rays of the swords by the National Museum have revealed that two of them had 'makers' marks' on their blades. Only ten such marks are known from Iron Age Britain, and are unique for each sword. Some archaeologists think these marks were a manufacturer's signature, but others believe they were part of an important, ritually significant vocabulary of symbols, possibly offering the user protection. The pelta (semi-circular shield) shapes used on the Llyn Cerrig Bach swords are often seen incorporated into Insular Celtic art of the period.

Mary Davis is Head of Archaeological Conservation at Amgueddfa Cymru – National Museum Wales

(**this page**) *The face of the Late Iron Age: this shield fitting, found at Tal-y-llyn in Gwynedd, dates from about AD 50-80. It probably represents a north Wales shield type, yet its decoration is influenced by the La Tène artistic style.*

(**opposite page**) *La Tène, a key site of the Iron Age in Europe, borders Lake Neuchâtel*

2 IRON AGE PEOPLES

ALL THE FINDS AT Llyn Cerrig Bach, apart from animal bones and fragments of wood, were made of metal. Some were of bronze (copper and tin alloy) and some of iron. Sir Cyril Fox had now confirmed that most of the significant items in the assemblage belonged to the European Iron Age, the period when iron tools and weapons became, literally, the cutting edge of new technology.

Iron had been used by people long before the so-called Iron Age. In Egypt, artefacts fashioned from meteoric iron have been dated to about 3500 BC. Iron smelted from ore was being used in Mesopotamia (ancient Iraq) as early as 2700 BC. However it was the production of high carbon iron, effectively steel, that made this metal supreme. Its hardness was the product of repeated tempering (heating to reduce brittleness), hammering on an anvil and cooling by quenching with water. These smithing skills were first developed in western Asia, especially by the Hittites of Anatolia (eastern Turkey) during the 1300s BC.

Ironworking skills were adopted or discovered in other parts of the world at different periods, so the term 'Iron Age' describes a period of technological development within a given region rather than some universal chronology.

Ironworking spread to Greece and from there through southern, central and then western Europe. Some small iron artefacts such as pins, awls and chisels were already being used as far to the west as Britain during the late Bronze Age, from about 1000 BC. By about 800 BC it could be said that a full-scale Iron Age had begun. Large amounts of bronze artefacts were still being produced, but iron was increasingly favoured for swords, spears and tools.

At the start of the Iron Age there was a highly skilled iron working culture in Central Europe. It was part of a series of cultural phases that archaeologists named 'Hallstatt', after a lakeside village in Upper Austria where a prehistoric burial ground was discovered in 1846. In Western Europe, the Hallstatt way of life took root around the River Danube, the Upper Rhine, the Alps and parts of France. Hallstatt society was based on trade and warfare. Its chieftains amassed wealth and prestige. Their smiths produced iron swords, daggers and axes.

From about 500 to 450 BC, until the Roman conquest of Gaul and Britain, another iron-working culture developed out of the Hallstatt world. It was named 'La Tène' after a typical site which was discovered at a lakeside village of that name in Switzerland – although the site's artefacts did not cover the whole period to which we now give its name.

Early styles of La Tène art (450-200 BC) were shared over large areas of temperate Europe, including Britain, although the various peoples did not have in common exactly the same culture, identity or beliefs. This was a high point of the culture that later historians called 'Celtic'. Its craft work in both bronze and iron as well as gold is splendid, featuring fluid, intricate motifs. Archaeologists refer to the late British and Irish manifestation of this art form as 'Insular' La Tène.

WHAT DO WE MEAN BY THE IRON AGE? HOW DID A NEW BREED OF METALWORKERS CHANGE THE EUROPEAN WAY OF LIFE?

Sparks from the forge

How did Iron Age smiths master the working of metals? **Tim Young** *introduces us to the techniques used in making iron and bronze to the high quality shown at Llyn Cerrig Bach*

The metal objects from Llyn Cerrig Bach demonstrate almost the entire repertoire of techniques used by the Iron Age metalworkers, in both iron and copper alloy. The chief copper alloy used in the Iron Age was bronze, a mixture of copper and tin.

Iron was the principal metal for everyday tools and implements. These are poorly represented at Llyn Cerrig Bach because of the mainly martial and equestrian nature of the assemblage, in which there is a dominance of decorative bronze. However ironwork includes a reaping hook and a sickle; there are also two examples of tongs, which serve to remind us of the array of tools involved in the creation of this wonderful metalwork.

The iron objects were produced by forging, with most of the working of the metal being undertaken 'hot'. By closing joins at high temperature, iron was able to be welded. The skills of the Iron Age blacksmith are amply demonstrated by the forge work on the gang chains and by the iron vehicle tyres, which had to be produced to such precise dimensions that on cooling they would shrink tightly onto the wooden wheels.

The weapons are the iron objects most likely to have had complex fabrication. Iron Age smiths had a variety of materials to work in – soft iron, hard high-phosphorus iron and heat-treatable carbon steels, probably distinguishable by the form of the so-called 'currency bars' in which they were traded (*see* p.62). Edge tools and weapons often show a careful choice of material and also the use of different materials for the individual components of the artefact.

Iron was also used for many of the bridle bits, some of which were straightforward iron objects, whilst others were coated with bronze, probably by brazing (a technique somewhat similar to soldering, in which molten copper alloy was used to coat or to join metal components), to appear similar to the bronze examples.

Objects made with bronze have two main methods of manufacture: casting and cold-working. Casting was usually undertaken using the lost wax process. A model of the object was made of beeswax and then coated in clay to form a mould. This was dried, then heated to melt the beeswax (which could be recycled). Bronze was melted in a crucible and poured into the mould. Once the metal had cooled and hardened, the mould was broken and the casting removed. In some instances, such as in the manufacture of the Llyn Cerrig Bach terrets, the casting would essentially be the finished object; for other items, such as the nave hoops, the casting would require further working. Some of the bridle bits with interlocking cast links were particularly complex castings.

Cold-working of the bronze entailed alternating episodes of working and

annealing (softening the metal by heating to relieve internal stresses). For sheet metal objects, a cast bronze ingot would be worked out into a sheet. Fashioning large convex shapes involved hammering to spread the metal either by 'sinking' – hammering the metal from the inside on a hard surface (for example in the creation of basal parts for cauldrons), or 'raising' – spreading the metal by hammering from the outside on a small anvil (the technique used to fashion the Llyn Cerrig Bach shield-boss mount).

Similar techniques, but employing a rounded punch instead of the hammer directly, were used to produce raised ornament: in 'repoussé' work, the sheet was worked from the rear (as for the nave hoops and the crescentic plaque) while in 'chasing' the metal was worked from the front (often to accentuate the repoussé work). In both cases, this would have been carried out against a firm, but yielding, support, perhaps of leather or pitch. The surface ornament on the bronze objects (such as the shield-boss mount) was produced by punching and by graving.

Sheet bronze artefacts were often fabricated and repaired by the use of copper alloy rivets, as evidenced by the Llyn Cerrig Bach horn and the cauldrons. Brazing was employed, in addition to riveting, to attach patches to one of the cauldrons and to the horn. The tubular rein-rings of some bridle bits would have been one of the most difficult types of sheet metal object to fashion.

Dr Tim Young *is an archaeometallurgist and experimental archaeologist, and founder of the GeoArch consultancy*

Archaeology in action: *the process of casting bronze (**opposite and above left**) and of brazing (**below**)*

A CELTIC CONUNDRUM

As early as about 500 BC the Ancient Greeks were calling the people living to their north, with whom they traded and fought, κελτοί [*Keltoi*] or Celts. The name may originally have referred to a specific tribe. The same term was picked up by the Romans as Celtae and applied chiefly to the Gauls, a people who had settled in northern Italy and France. To the classical world, 'Celts' signified the 'other peoples', the 'peoples who are not like us'. Archaeology however reveals that in reality these were no barbarians, but skilled and sophisticated peoples.

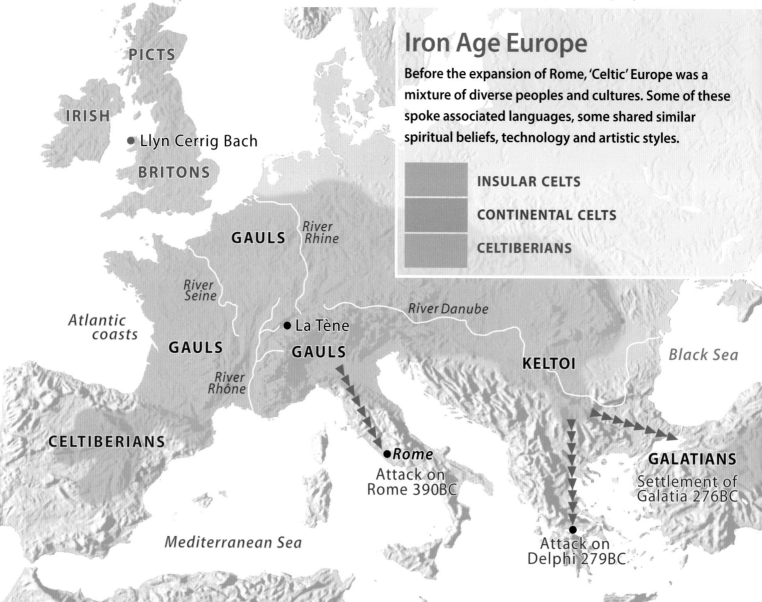

The language chart:
- GALLO-BRYTHONIC
  - BRYTHONIC — WELSH, CORNISH, BRETON
  - GAULISH
- GOIDELIC — MANX, SCOTTISH GAELIC, OLD IRISH → IRISH
- LEPONTIC
- HISPANO-CELTIC

BC | AD

The language of the Iron Age Britons was a precursor to Welsh. It was related to other Celtic languages.

Iron Age Europe

Before the expansion of Rome, 'Celtic' Europe was a mixture of diverse peoples and cultures. Some of these spoke associated languages, some shared similar spiritual beliefs, technology and artistic styles.

INSULAR CELTS
CONTINENTAL CELTS
CELTIBERIANS

PICTS

IRISH

Llyn Cerrig Bach

BRITONS

GAULS

River Rhine

River Seine

Atlantic coasts

La Tène

GAULS

GAULS

River Danube

River Rhône

KELTOI

Black Sea

CELTIBERIANS

Rome
Attack on Rome 390BC

GALATIANS
Settlement of Galatia 276BC

Mediterranean Sea

Attack on Delphi 279BC

The term 'Celtic' was increasingly adopted from the 1700s onwards by historians and linguists, such as the Welsh polymath Edward Lhuyd (1660–1709), and ever since it has had a wide variety of applications.

The term is used in archaeology to describe the so-called La Tène culture and its artistic expression (*see* p.19). It is also sometimes used to describe all the Iron Age peoples who were influenced by these cultural developments. This 'Celtic' world stretched at its greatest extent from Galicia (in Spain) to Galatia (in Turkey), from northern Scotland to northern Italy. Amongst archaeologists, in recent years, there has been some shift of focus from the peoples of Central Europe to those of the Atlantic coasts, when considering the ways in which Iron Age cultures were transmitted and assimilated.

The search for a Celtic identity is one which concerns linguists as well as archaeologists. One family of Indo-European languages is described as Celtic. It has been suggested that its origins lay around the valleys of the Rivers Rhône and Saône, in Switzerland and France. More recently it has been proposed that these are better described as 'Atlantic' languages, perhaps evolving in the Iberian peninsula. How, when and by what route these proto-Celtic languages became spoken in the British Isles is a matter of great debate, a puzzle that remains unresolved. Ancient Celtic languages included Gaulish, Goidelic and Brythonic. The versions of these which have survived into modern times include Welsh, Cornish and Breton in one group, and Irish, Scottish Gaelic and Manx in another.

The term 'Celtic' has also been used in relation to those cultures in the far west of Europe which survived the Germanic invasions following the collapse of the Roman empire. The form of early Christianity which took root in Britain, the first Welsh poetry, the magnificent metalwork and manuscripts of medieval Ireland, have all been styled as Celtic.

In more recent times we also use the word 'Celtic' to describe the eighteenth to twenty-first century cultural and political revivals which took place in Scotland, Wales, Ireland, Man, Cornwall, Brittany and Galicia. A trawl of the internet today reveals the word Celtic further applied to a bewildering variety of commercial names, mystical cults, design motifs, clothing and jewellery items, styles of music and historical romances featured in novels or television series.

Small wonder that many archaeologists and historians have become wary of terms such as 'the Celtic Iron Age'. They fear that the blanket term tends to conflate the various uses of the word. They are also concerned that it gives a misleading impression of a cultural or political unity that never existed.

There were of course many shared cultural and linguistic links across Europe in the Iron Age. For example, Celtic elements have survived in many modern European place names. However there was also great diversity, even within smaller regions. In Britain alone the archaeological evidence suggests a complex mosaic of regional identities and variances in the ways that societies developed and changed.

Despite all these perceived shortcomings, some people feel that 'Celtic' remains valid as a shorthand term, which brings together certain cultural and linguistic elements in Iron Age Europe. In this book we, like the Greeks and Romans, refer to the people of Llyn Cerrig Bach and their cousins elsewhere in Europe as Celts — always bearing in mind that it is never a precise term referring to a single people.

FROM ANCIENT TIMES TO THE PRESENT, THE WORD 'CELTIC' HAS BEEN USED TO DESCRIBE A COMPLEX AND FOREVER CHANGING MIXTURE OF CULTURES, LANGUAGES AND PEOPLES

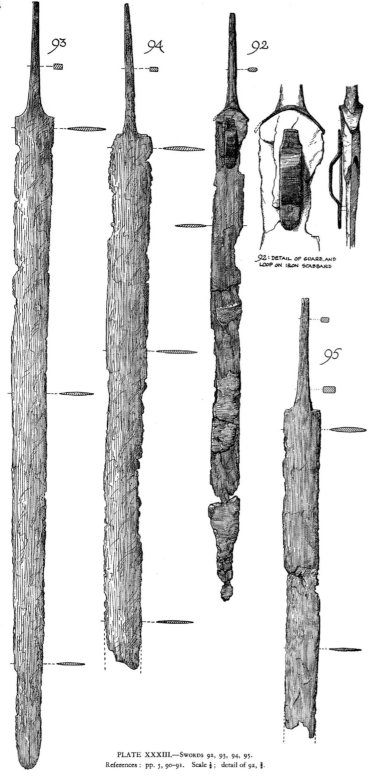

93 94 92

92: DETAIL OF GUARD, AND LOOP ON IRON SCABBARD

95

PLATE XXXIII.—Swords 92, 93, 94, 95.
References : pp. 5, 90–91. Scale ⅓; detail of 92, ⅔.

Llyn Cerrig Bach swords : archaeological evidence provides us with the most reliable information about Iron Age Anglesey

KEYS TO THE PAST

The cultures, languages, beliefs and technologies of the Iron Age Celts were spread by movements of peoples and ideas. Sometimes these people were raiders, traders or settlers; sometimes they were refugees. However social developments in Britain are far more likely to have been shaped by internal tribal conflicts than by attacks or invasions from outsiders.

Seeing the large number of hillforts constructed in Britain during this period, archaeologists once believed that at some point there must have been a single large-scale invasion of the British Isles by Celts from mainland Europe. However it is now widely believed that Celtic cultural ideas were absorbed into Britain as a gradual and partial process, through trade, settlement and other contacts over many centuries. For instance, even in southeast England where 'Belgic invasions' were quite convincingly identified up to 40 years ago, the current view is that close contacts were maintained across the Channel, whence new ideas and fashions were imported with perhaps a few immigrants, but that no aggressive invasion took place.

The people of Britain as a whole were already known as Britons – not Celts – to the Greeks and Romans. Amongst themselves, they would not have recognised a common identity prior to the Roman conquest. They were mostly descended from indigenous or long-standing inhabitants, but had absorbed cultures from continental Europe and its Atlantic coasts over the millennia. By the Iron Age they shared many religious beliefs and social customs with the wider Celtic world.

How do we know about the Iron Age Celts? Our most reliable source is archaeology, which can give us insights into their technology, their social structure, their trading patterns. We can see for ourselves the remains of their wealthy *oppida* (fortified towns) in southern Gaul, or the roundhouses and heavily defended hillforts of Britain. Aerial photography reveals their ancient field patterns. We can see exquisitely fashioned bronze hand mirrors, or gold ornaments called torcs, worn on the necks and arms of the nobles. We can see fine swords, spears and shields – it is sites such as Llyn Cerrig Bach which provide us with material evidence.

We can also turn to contemporary writers. There were none from Britain which was a pre-literate society, passing down information through an oral tradition. We have to rely instead on Greek and Roman historians and geographers. Many of these drew upon the writings of a Greek philosopher called Posidonius (*c*.135-51 BC), who had travelled amongst the Gauls. His original work does not survive, but it was taken up in the work of Diodorus Siculus (*fl*. 60-30 BC) and Strabo (*c*.64 BC – *c*.AD 24).

The best known chronicler of the Celts is Julius Caesar (100-44 BC), the Roman general who conquered Gaul and briefly invaded southern Britain in 55 and 54 BC. He had faced both Gauls and Britons in battle and campaigned in their lands. He required accurate knowledge of people, places and customs in order to gain effective political control.

Pliny the Elder (AD 23-79), who died during the eruption of Vesuvius, described Celtic religious rituals. It is in the *Annals* of the Roman historian Tacitus (AD 56-117) that we get our closest approach to the location and people of Llyn Cerrig Bach. He vividly describes the Romans' first assault on Anglesey ('Mona Insula') in AD 60. (*see* p.44)

Julius Caesar admires chariot warfare in Britain

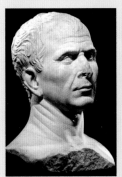

"The chariot drivers gradually withdraw from the battle and position the chariots in such a way that should the fighting men be overwhelmed by enemy numbers, they can quickly return to them. They therefore combine the mobility of the cavalry with the solidity of infantry in battle, and become so skilled in their use through training and daily practice that they can even control galloping horses on steep and dangerous slopes."

Julius Caesar, The Gallic War IV, 33

Pliny the Elder describes a Druidic ritual in Gaul

"The Druids (which is the name they give to their magicians) consider nothing more sacred than mistletoe and the tree that it grows upon, so long as it is an oak. ... Mistletoe is actually very rare on oak trees, and when it is found it is gathered with great ceremony. In the first place, the collection must take place on the sixth day of the moon. This day is the beginning of their months, their years and their centuries (the latter lasting thirty years). ... A priest dressed in white climbs the tree, cuts the mistletoe with a golden sickle and catches it on a white cloak."

Pliny the Elder, Natural History XVI, 9

Classical authors do provide us with fascinating information, but it cannot always be relied on. When describing 'barbarians', Roman writers were often sensationalist, reporting anecdotes or hearsay. The Romans had a political agenda, too. After all, the Celts were often their enemies. We also have to bear in mind that what was true in Gaul or southern Britain might not have necessarily been the case in what is now north Wales.

Another key to understanding the Iron Age Celts is by referral back from later sources. Aspects of earlier 'pagan' Celtic culture can still be traced as sub-texts in many tales and epics from the oral tradition which were first written down in the Middle Ages. Of course the passing of the centuries and the cultural context in which these stories emerged corrupted the original stories, but the ancient world can be glimpsed here and there. An Irish manuscript of the twelfth century, the *Táin bó Cúailnge*, takes us straight back to the cattle raiding and heroics of the Irish Iron Age. The medieval Welsh manuscript of the *Mabinogi* includes fabulous tales of hunting, warfare and magical transformations that clearly have ancient roots in the pagan world of the Iron Age Britons.

AS WELL AS ARCHAEOLOGICAL EVIDENCE WE HAVE THE WORDS OF CLASSICAL WRITERS — BUT JUST HOW RELIABLE ARE THEY?

Anglesey in the Iron Age

What kind of a place was Anglesey at the time of the Llyn Cerrig Bach deposits?
George Smith considers archaeological evidence from the island's settlements

Recent aerial photography, geophysical survey and excavations confirm that Anglesey was densely farmed and settled during the Iron Age.

Many examples of settlement from the later first millennium BC have survived into modern times. If these remains are fewer in number than those on the nearby mainland – despite the superior quality of the island's soil – it must be because subsequent intensive agriculture has destroyed the evidence. The Anglesey landscape was particularly affected by the clearances and improvements of the eighteenth and nineteenth centuries.

Iron Age Anglesey was characterised by a mixture of settlement types. Some of these continued to be occupied during the Roman period, with only slight changes due to wider trade and cultural contacts and the introduction of a market economy with coinage as a medium of exchange.

Some small groups of Iron Age buildings lay within ditched and banked enclosures, which might be rectilinear or curvilinear in design. The nine such enclosed farmsteads which are known were concentrated in the areas of better soil, chiefly in the south and east of the island, and each probably belonged to one extended family group.

Some scattered dwellings and some closely set groups of houses remained open and undefended. These reflect a different type of social structure and possibly a difference of land-holding and use. They are perhaps more like a village. At Tŷ Mawr (*right*), near South Stack, there were about fifty such houses with associated arable fields, demonstrating a peaceful and stable society.

Stability must have depended on the presence of accepted territories maintained or overseen by some central authority, located at this period in hillforts or other well defended enclosures, although it is probable that not all the structures which survive today were contemporary. Hillforts housed only a very small portion of the population. They must also have acted as places of refuge in occasional times of need: this would have been the case at Caer y Twr on Ynys Gybi (Holy Island), a fort which is very large in area but has no evidence of occupation. Hillforts may have also served as secure stores for grain and possibly as communal meeting and market places.

Construction of the forts demanded large inputs of labour and communal involvement, whether voluntary or as a due to an 'overlord' or perhaps a warrior clan. The ability to acquire weapons or to employ blacksmiths indicates some transfer of resources between the farming population and the overlord.

Most of the domestic objects from excavated houses are basic items such as querns, mortars and spindle whorls. In all the types of settlement neither the artefacts discovered nor the design and size of houses reveal any great differences in status or individual wealth. If such status was present, then it must have been expressed by means of personal adornment or the acquisition of fine weapons, some of foreign origin, and other decorated equipment such as the items found at Llyn Cerrig Bach.

Although the excavated remains of farming settlements may suggest to us a personal life of great poverty, this is no doubt misleading. Organic objects of wood, bone, horn and textile have not survived. Iron was recyclable so would rarely be discarded. Pottery is absent but must have had its wooden or horn equivalents.

The substantial size and construction of defended sites means that most are still recognisable today. Although all may not have been occupied at the same time, their distribution can tell us something about territories on the island. Such territories require boundaries, usually geographical features such as rivers. These features are likely to have survived as boundaries into historical times and possibly formed the basis of the medieval land divisions known as commotes. Each of the larger enclosures would have overseen an area of about 115 square kilometres (45 sq.mi.), rather less for Ynys Gybi.

Anglesey experienced some influence from Ireland, but less than, say, Pembrokeshire. The settlements and artefacts of Anglesey are similar to those of the adjoining mainland and there is no evidence that it was culturally separate.

George Smith is a Senior Archaeologist with the Gwynedd Archaeological Trust

This Iron Age farming settlement, Tŷ Mawr on Holyhead Mountain near South Stack, is made up of undefended roundhouses and livestock pens

3 WAYS OF LIFE

WHAT WOULD THE Iron Age Celts have looked like? The classical writers describe the Celts' pride in their appearance and their delight in jewellery such as gold torcs (neck bands) and in body decoration. Hair was worn long by men and women, and often plaited. Men wore moustaches. Sometimes hair was bleached, or spiked with a wash of lime before battle. Such fashions may have been followed in some parts of Britain, but customs must have varied from one region to the next. For example, no Iron Age gold torcs have been found in Wales.

The stereotypical Celt, according to the southern Europeans, was brave, boastful, given to heroics, quick to anger and a fierce fighter. Women enjoyed high social status and power. For example it was Boudicca or Buddug, queen of the eastern British Iceni tribe, who led the uprising against the Romans in AD 60, at the time when the legions in the west were engaged in the conquest of Anglesey. She burned down the city of London. Tacitus has her say, 'We Britons are used to women commanders in war.' (*Annals* XIV, 35)

Tribes probably developed from smaller hillfort communities during the Middle to Late Iron Age. At this time, there would have been many competing sub-tribes and changing tribal structures. By the first century AD the principal tribes of mid- and north Wales were the Ordovices (southwards from Snowdonia), the Gangani (perhaps a sub-tribe occupying the Llŷn peninsula) and the Deceangli, whose territory was focussed around the Vale of Clwyd. There is no clue to the name of the tribe or sub-tribe in Anglesey, but Tacitus tells us that at the time of the Roman conquest many refugees from the fighting in eastern and southern Britain fled westwards to Snowdonia and Anglesey.

Iron Age societies were local and diverse. From the evidence we have it is difficult to propose a single model for Iron Age society across Britain. A tribal territory might be ruled by a chieftain or, in some areas during the late Iron Age, by a king or queen. A ruler's power and prestige depended on the size of their territory and on the number of nobles who were loyal to them. There was no ensured succession and no permanent centres of royal power. Social elites made alliances and vied with each other for control.

At the time of the Roman invasion these powerful elites provided tribes with their leading warriors and their priests, called Druids. Strabo describes the other priestly classes as seers or soothsayers, and as bards, who gave the tribe its oral history, through poetry and music. Druids were also people of learning who served as envoys to other tribes, as lawmakers, arbitrators, educators and healers. They were treated with great respect and a chief Druid could silence a king or queen. Tacitus confirms their presence on Anglesey.

Anglesey's archaeology offers little direct evidence about social classes in the Iron Age. The great majority of the population would have been farmers or labourers, with some workers no doubt specialising as traders, craft workers or smiths. The latter enjoyed a highly respected social position in Iron Age society.

The Iron Age settlements on the island do not reveal great variation in personal wealth but the building of some establishments must have demanded more labour than others, and we do know that by the time Llyn Cerrig Bach was at the height of its use, warfare, weapons and horses were matters of great importance.

LATE IRON AGE SOCIETIES WERE TRIBAL — WITH RULERS, DRUIDS, WARRIORS, FARMERS, TRADERS AND SMITHS ...

WARRIORS & HEROES

The Llyn Cerrig Bach treasure reveals a society in which weapons were revered. Our present knowledge of Celtic warfare comes from finds of arms and armour, and also from the portrayal of the Celts in classical literature and sculpture.

The Iron Age Celts placed great value on personal combat between champions. Medieval Irish literature harks back to the martial ideals of the Iron Age in its description of the heroic warrior Cú Chulainn, a cunning cattle raider and the champion of Ulster. He was famed for his terrifying battle frenzy.

The true genius of Celtic warriors lay in raiding and skirmishing. Unlike the Romans, they were not organised as full-time standing armies – come harvest time they would be needed back on the land. The role of the warrior in Anglesey life during the Iron Age or the Romano-British period remains unknown. For them, warfare was probably sporadic and fighting an occasional occupation. As the Iron Age advanced there was an increase in tribes mustering against a common enemy and fighting pitched battles, a process accelerated by the Romans' advance northwards through Gaul and Britain.

Celtic warriors had a love of horses. When the tribes later came under Roman rule, they were often recruited into the cavalry. Leading warriors rode to battle in chariots pulled by two small, tough horses – as the evidence of Llyn Cerrig Bach suggests (*see* p.52). A driver controlled the horses. The warrior hurled javelins while charging enemy lines. He might show reckless bravado by running along the pole of the chariot to stand between the horses. The chariot would then return to the ranks, and the warrior would dismount to fight on foot.

We cannot be sure how the warriors who visited Llyn Cerrig Bach actually dressed. Celtic fighters are generally portrayed as wearing tunics and chequered breeches, or sometimes fighting naked in contempt of the enemy's spears. Helmets and shirts of mail might be worn by elite warriors – in fact armour

(left) Shields were symbols of power and status. The ceremonial Battersea shield dates from the period between 350 and 50 BC.

(opposite) The Celts were known throughout the ancient world for their fury in battle.

made of meshed iron links was probably a Celtic invention. However most warriors fought light and bare-headed.

At the period of the Llyn Cerrig Bach deposits, shields (*see* p.55) were generally of a long, flattened oval shape. Wood and hide have rotted away over the ages, so the only remnants are metal parts made of iron or bronze. These include ribs and bosses designed to strengthen the shield. The boss (a central knob) covered the hand grip of the shield, and the Llyn Cerrig Bach mount offers a fine example. The Celts made some shields purely for ceremonial or votive use. The famous Battersea shield, recovered from the River Thames in London, was entirely faced with a decorative sheet of bronze and studs of red glass.

The most valued weapon of the Celtic warrior was an iron sword, often with a bronze grip and mountings. It might be sheathed in a decorated scabbard attached to a chain belt. Of the handles, only the metal parts have survived. Blade design varied over the ages both in length and width and the eleven sword remains found at Llyn Cerrig Bach were clearly made at quite different dates. Other Celtic hand weapons included daggers and slings. Iron-headed spears with shafts of two metres or more were used for stabbing or for ceremonial use. Smaller spears were used for throwing.

In troubled times warriors could withdraw into hill forts or promontory forts, which might be defended by earth and stone ramparts, timber gates and palisades. Many such forts were already in use as refuges and settlements long before the time of Llyn Cerrig Bach, and some continued to be used long afterwards.

CELTIC WARRIORS TAUNTED THE ENEMY BEFORE BATTLE. TACITUS REPORTS HOW THE SOUND AND FURY OF FIGHTING MEN AND WILD WOMEN SENT A SHIVER DOWN THE SPINE OF EVEN THE MOST HARDENED LEGIONARIES WHEN THE ROMANS INVADED ANGLESEY

ROUNDHOUSE & HEARTH

Iron Age settlements were built all over the land, forming a mosaic of individual farms and hillforts. They were linked by tracks, causeways, fords, wooden bridges and by trading routes. Although we may think that the Romans were the first to build engineered roads, one discovered near Shrewsbury in 2011 was found to predate the Roman conquest by a century or so. It was built of timber, mud and cobbles. Goods were also transported by boat along rivers and by sea.

Around the dwellings of a settlement there might be outbuildings, including workshops, livestock pens, fields and paddocks.

In Britain and Ireland the typical design for a dwelling was a roundhouse. Building materials varied according to local availability, and included timber, earth, stone or wattle-and-daub – interwoven staves plastered with clay. Beams supported a high conical roof which was thatched with reed or grasses.

The original dimensions can be gauged from post-holes identified by archaeologists, or by the remains of stone walls, such as those of the 'Tŷ Mawr' huts still visible on the slopes of Holyhead Mountain. Typical measurements on Anglesey give an internal diameter of 6 to 8 metres. Archaeologists have been able to clarify likely building techniques during modern experimental reconstructions. The nearest of these to Llyn Cerrig Bach have been erected at Llanddeusant, next to Llynnon Mill. These impressive roundhouses were constructed by Ancient Arts of Degannwy and opened to the public in 2007.

Iron Age dwellings and outbuildings were used for cooking, eating, storage, weaving and sleeping. The perimeter areas could be divided into radial cubicles. The floor was of beaten earth and at its centre was a smouldering hearth, its logs supported by firedogs. These could be prestigious decorative items – an example from the first century AD, found at Capel Garmon near Llanrwst, is one of the finest pieces of ironwork of its age.

The settlements would have been noisy with the sound of barking hounds and farm animals. Livestock included shorthorn cattle, small pigs, goats and sheep (ancestors of today's Soay breed). Hunting in the forests provided additional sources of food. Meat was preserved by salting, drying or smoking. There are surprisingly few indications of fishing, but the evidence would be elusive in any case.

The fields were treated with manure. They were prepared for cultivation with an ard (a pointed wooden pole used to scratch a narrow furrow), or with a development of the ard, a simple iron-tipped ploughshare. A broad blade that could turn the soil was a Roman invention. Barley and wheat were grown in the fields. The crops were harvested with sickles, and grain was milled by hand using stone grinders called querns. Of course many crops and foods that are familiar to us today had yet to be introduced into the British Isles. Hazelnuts, berries and apples were gathered and honey was used as a sweetener.

Across Iron Age Europe, Celtic tribal leaders were famous for their love of feasting and their prodigious drinking. Large and beautiful tankards like those from Trawsfynydd are witness to the importance of hospitality. The coming of the Romans introduced wine. Feasts were held to mark victories and other important events, and the lavish generosity of a chieftain enhanced his prestige and political power amongst his followers.

Grain was ground into flour by hand, using a quern of rough stone

COOKING CAULDRONS SIMMERED, HANGING FROM CHAINS
OVER THE FIRE. SMOKE ROSE TO FILL THE ROOF SPACE
AND ESCAPE THROUGH THE THATCH

The island economy

How did the people of Anglesey make a living in the Iron Age?
Andrew Davidson looks at farming, resources and trade

One of the more functional finds from the Llyn Cerrig Bach hoard is an iron sickle. The inclusion of a simple agricultural tool amongst the splendour of chariots, swords and harness fittings is a reminder of the importance of farming to Iron Age Anglesey.

The island's agricultural economy was a mixed one. Grains of corn, preserved through accidental charring, have been found on a number of sites. These show that there were two varieties of wheat being grown, emmer and spelt, as well as barley. Spelt tended to replace emmer at this time because it was more reliable, particularly on marginal land. Wheat was being grown on areas of heath and grassland, while barley was grown on wetter and heavier soils. Oats do not appear to have been seriously cultivated until during or after the Roman period. Weed seeds found with the grain suggests that ploughing was undertaken with an ard, which, unlike a mould-board plough, only tilled the ground, and did not turn the soil over to bury weeds. The soils of lowland Anglesey, superior to those of the mountainous mainland, suggest that the island could provide a surplus over and above its internal needs.

Sheep, goats and pigs were raised on the farms. Cattle were kept for traction, meat and hides, whilst horses were typically used for non-agricultural purposes, and were of higher status.

Most raw materials needed for manufacture were derived locally. Many roundhouses had walls built of stone, and where identifiable this seems to have been collected from fields or other readily available local sources. The removal of field stone had the added bonus of clearing land for cultivation. There is little evidence for large-scale quarrying. Some building stones, however, were carefully shaped, as, for example, a tall pillar with a tenon joint found at Holyhead. That this was no exception is shown by the recovery of similar stones over a hundred years earlier. These are thought to have supported a granary.

Bowls used as mortars could be made from various types of stone, but querns, the stones used for grinding grain, were from more particular sources. There was a wide trade in quern stones. Some of these were highly decorated with incised patterns. Medium-sized stones are commonly found with holes drilled through them. These had many potential uses, in particular for holding down the warp on a vertical loom, or as fishing weights. Slightly larger examples may have held down thatch. On a smaller scale are the round spindle whorls, fashioned from a wide variety of materials and also often decorated.

Large round pits are often discovered and these are thought to have been used for the extraction and puddling of clay. There is considerable evidence for the construction of cob (clay mixed with straw) roundhouses on Anglesey. Clay was also used to produce daub, usually applied to wattle hurdles to create non-load-bearing divisions. Timber was a widespread natural resource, and pollen analysis has revealed the presence of mature woodland in many parts of Anglesey in this period.

Pottery was not produced in Anglesey during the Iron Age. Only one sherd of any kind has been found, at Holyhead – probably 'Malvernian' ware (from the Malvern Hills). Pottery making was re-introduced to the island by the Romans. However a coarse type of ceramic, called *briquetage*, has been found at Iron

Age sites. It was used for vessels with a flared rim, which were used to dry salt originating from brine springs in the Cheshire Plain. The salt was subsequently transported in the vessels, and found its way to some settlements in Anglesey. Salt was vital for the preservation of foodstuffs, and the identification of vessels from Cheshire is a good indication of external trade.

The extraction and processing of copper at Parys Mountain, which took place during the early Bronze Age, had ceased by the early Iron Age, when there was a reduction in metal production throughout Britain. The subsequent increase in iron production is poorly evidenced in Anglesey, though considerable evidence has been found in Merioneth, where bog ores were smelted, and wood for charcoal was in plentiful supply. There is slightly more evidence for smithing in Anglesey, which is necessary to turn the processed ore into finished tools. The iron bars from Llyn Cerrig Bach were part of a sophisticated trade in iron ready for smithing (*see* p.62). Coins were not used in Wales until the Roman period, and the exchange of goods would have been through barter or through the payment of dues in the form of food, goods or labour services to the rulers.

Andrew Davidson is *Chief Archaeologist of the Gwynedd Archaeological Trust*

The defended settlement at Caer Lêb, near Brynsiencyn, continued to flourish economically after the Roman conquest

Fine examples of Insular La Tène art:
— *a decorative head from a bucket (Aylesford c.75-25 BC),*
— *a bronze hand mirror from Desborough (c.50 BC – AD 50),*
— *(below) reconstruction of a ceremonial crown, Cerrigydrudion (c.400 BC).*

SKILL AND BEAUTY

Under the influence of the La Tène culture from the fifth century BC, there was a flowering of artistic and technologically advanced design across Europe. Trade increased cultural contact between the continental Celts and the peoples of the Mediterranean and western Asia. The Celts transformed these influences into unique forms of expression. These affected to a degree the insular cultures of Britain and Ireland. The Llyn Cerrig Bach treasure includes fine examples.

La Tène period art still fascinates us today. It is characterised by vitality, by intricate design and flowing, swirling patterns. It manages to create harmony whilst tending to avoid symmetrical designs. There are sometimes lively depictions of animals and of powerful, stylised heads of humans and gods. All sorts of artefacts of metal, stone, pottery, horn and wood might be ornamented in this way – helmets, scabbards, harnesses, chariot fittings, carts, flagons, cauldrons, firedogs, hand mirrors and jewellery such as torcs, brooches and pins for fastening cloaks.

Specialist craft workers such as goldsmiths and jewellers produced the most precious items, such as the splendid torcs which signified high status in many parts of the Celtic world. One spectacular treasure hoard found at Snettisham in Norfolk contained over 70 torcs and many more fragments.

Torc finds are not a feature of Wales at this time, but collars of bronze and brass were worn in the first and early second centuries AD. A ceremonial helmet or crown (previously identified wrongly as a hanging bowl) was found at Cerrigydrudion, in the county of Conwy. It dates from about 400 BC and is elaborately decorated in the Early La Tène style.

Less high status craft items such as pottery, wood, leather, horn or basketry were also made in Iron Age Europe, for everyday use. Hand made pottery was made by shaping vessels from coils or slabs of clay and was fired in a pit or a bonfire. However almost no pottery from this period has been found in north Wales. More sophisticated wheel-thrown pottery was introduced into some parts of southern and eastern England from the later second century BC onwards.

The making of cloth was carried out in the home. Flax was grown to make linen, but the most common fabric was made of wool. Wool was spun into yarn by hand, using a drop-spindle. As a round weight, or whorl, was spun around, the spinner's thumb and forefinger twisted the attached fibre into thread. The yarn was woven on a tall upright loom. The warp (vertical) threads were kept taut with weights, while the weft (horizontal) threads were passed between them and pushed into place with combs of bone or horn. Natural dyes included madder for red, weld for yellow and woad for blue. Brightly coloured and embroidered clothes were another aspect of Celtic finery.

(right) These figures adorn the Gundestrup cauldron, a fine silver vessel of the first century BC discovered in a Danish bog. Its decorations portray rituals of the late La Tène period, including warriors blowing the carnyx, a long, thin war trumpet. Its mouth was fashioned to look like a boar, a serpent, a wolf or some other totemic creature. The instrument was designed to be held upright as it was played, ringing out over the tumult of battle.

(below) A Celtic masterpiece in gold — a torc from Snettesham, c.75 BC.

LA TÈNE IMAGERY SEEMS TO BE CHARGED WITH THE SPIRIT OF LIFE AND IS ROOTED IN CELTIC RELIGIOUS AND SPIRITUAL BELIEFS. AT THE SAME TIME IT EXPRESSES THE LOVE OF DISPLAY AND ORNAMENT BY THE RULING CLASS, WHO FLAUNTED THEIR WEALTH TO DEMONSTRATE POLITICAL POWER AND PERSONAL PRESTIGE

REALMS OF THE SPIRIT

Many modern European geographical names derive from Celtic gods and goddesses. The peoples of the Iron Age honoured local and tribal deities, earth goddesses and gods of the sky and sun. Some deities seem to have been shared across wider areas of Britain, Ireland and continental Europe, and have come down to us under a variety of names.

Many fascinating references to these deities survive from the Roman and the medieval periods. These may not always accurately reflect the original perceptions of these gods, but when we read of the terrifying Irish goddess known as the Morrigan flying over battlefields in the form of a crow, or in Wales of Llew of the Strong Hand with his spear and sling, we are perhaps approaching the mindset of the Iron Age.

The soul never dies ...

"One of [the Druids'] principal beliefs is that the soul never dies, but after death passes from one body to another, which, they think, helps greatly to exalt men's courage, by robbing death of its terrors.

"They also teach many things relating to the stars and their motions, the magnitude of the world, the nature of things and the power and prerogatives of the immortal gods."

Julius Caesar, The Gallic War, 51 BC

An interesting find from Hen-dŷ farm near Llanfair Pwllgwynyll is a stone head, which may well represent a local deity and have been used in religious rituals. This powerful, rather unsettling carving in sandstone – now displayed in Oriel Ynys Môn, Llangefni – cannot be dated with certainty, but it may belong to the Late Iron Age or the Romano-British period.

Heads were considered to be the location of the soul, and to have sacred significance. In Welsh mythology, as elaborated in the *Mabinogi*, the mortally wounded king Bendigeidfran orders his followers to cut off his head. They eventually bury it under White Hill in London. Celtic warriors were said to cut off the heads of defeated enemies and display them in their houses.

(above) Does the enigmatic Hen-dŷ stone head represent an Anglesey deity?

(below) This figure on the Gundestrup cauldron may show Cernunnos, the horned god of Celtic mythology. A torc is held in his right hand.

Springs and wells were sacred, as they have been in many cultures around the world. On Anglesey they were later adopted by Christian saints and were revered as places of healing, soothsaying or magic into modern times. Witchcraft rituals were recorded at Llaneilan's 'cursing well' as late as 1921.

Trees were at the heart of Druidic ritual – the name *derwydd*, Druid, is linked to *derwen*, meaning 'oak'. No sooner had the Roman legions invaded Anglesey than they were ordered to destroy the island's sacred groves, presumably in an attempt to break the political and spiritual power of the Druids.

Whilst nature provided many sacred sites, such as Anglesey's oak groves and lakes like Llyn Cerrig Bach, some shrines and sanctuaries in the Celtic world were man-made. These were ditched enclosures where rituals were conducted and offerings made to the gods. In Wales there is little evidence for such shrines during the Iron Age, but there are shrines and temples from the Roman period.

Animals, birds and fishes were closely allied to the supernatural, and surrounded by taboos. Some of these creatures appear in La Tène ornament and in later literature, where physical transformations between the worlds of gods, humans and animals are common.

Druidism is described by Roman writers and it is hard to assess the accuracy of their reports, but it is clear that Druids were versed in ritual so it would seem likely that they presided 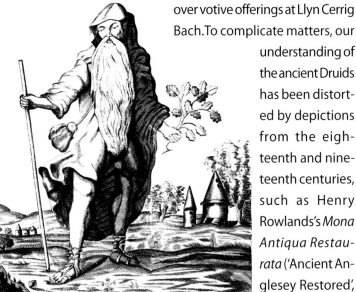 over votive offerings at Llyn Cerrig Bach. To complicate matters, our understanding of the ancient Druids has been distorted by depictions from the eighteenth and nineteenth centuries, such as Henry Rowlands's *Mona Antiqua Restaurata* ('Ancient Anglesey Restored', 1723), and by the romantically inspired 'Druidical' rites for eisteddfodau devised by Edward Williams ('Iolo Morganwg') in 1792.

Tacitus' description of the Roman invasion of Anglesey in AD 60 does refer to the Druids, grouped in a circle on the banks of the Menai Strait with hands raised in prayer. He also tells of black-robed women moving amongst the ranks of the warriors like the Furies, brandishing torches and uttering curses. Might these have been priestesses of some cult?

Tacitus describes the Druidic altars as being slaked with blood. This might well have been the Roman equivalent of modern tabloid journalism, and equally hypocritical since Rome itself had only abandoned human sacrifice early in the first century BC. However archaeological evidence does confirm that ritual killings and both animal and human sacrifice were practised in the Iron Age (*see* p.41), with much of the evidence coming from bogs similar to those surrounding Llyn Cerrig Bach.

THE LANDSCAPE AND THE NATURAL WORLD WERE BRIMMING WITH SPIRITUAL MEANING

The Lady of the Lake

To many people in Britain, the image of a sword being hurled into a lake immediately recalls the legends of King Arthur and his great sword Excalibur (known to the Welsh as Caledfwlch). Arthur, if he existed at all, would have been a British war leader who fought the Saxon invaders in the late fifth or early sixth century AD.

Later in the Middle Ages, references to Arthur resurfaced in the literature of Wales and were transmitted to England and continental Europe. *Le Morte d'Arthur* by Sir Thomas Mallory (c.1405-71) portrays Arthur as a medieval king, and describes how Bedivere (the Welsh Bedwyr) returned the sword Excalibur to the custody of the Lady of the Lake when Arthur died. This story was adapted into a moving poem by Alfred, Lord Tennyson (1809-92), the *Idylls of the King*. Here we have travelled a long way from the Iron Age and Llyn Cerrig Bach, yet this poem shows how the powerful symbolism of the sword and the lake has survived intact down the ages, and can still move us today.

Then quickly rose Sir Bedivere, and ran,
And, leaping down the ridges lightly, plunged
Among the bulrush beds, and clutched the sword,
And strongly wheeled and threw it. The great brand
Made lightnings in the splendour of the moon,
And flashing round and round, and whirled in an arch,
Shot like a streamer of the northern morn,
Seen where the moving isles of winter shock
By night, with noises of the Northern Sea.
So flashed and fell the brand Excalibur:
But ere he dipt the surface, rose an arm
Clothed in white samite, mystic, wonderful,
And caught him by the hilt, and brandished him
Three times, and drew him under in the mere.

'The Passing of Arthur'
from *Idylls of the King* (1856–85)
Alfred, Lord Tennyson

THE WATER'S EDGE

Humans seem to have a fascination with the interface between dry land and water. We stand at the edges of lakes and throw in pebbles to make ripples, or skip flat stones across the surface. We stare into the depths and marvel at reflections. We describe stepping stones or bridges as metaphors for our lives. We throw coins into 'wishing' wells or fountains. At the seashore we watch the procession of endless waves. We feel serenity when the waters are calm, and fear or excitement when they are wild.

These elemental feelings might explain why human beings of many cultures around the world, and at different times in history, have carried out rituals such as burial, sacrifice or votive offering at the margins of pools, lakes and bogs, by rivers and seashores.

An example far from Europe is the Sacred Cenote or pool at Chichen Itza in Mexico, where precious artefacts made of gold, jade and obsidian as well as human sacrifices were thrown into the water by the Maya, as offerings to the rain god Chaac.

In Arthurian legend the magical land of eternal rest and healing is an island called Avalon; in Irish myth the timeless paradise of Tír na nÓg lies beyond the western sea. Both lands are islands, where solid land is surrounded by mist, by fluidity of time, by ebb and flow. Britain too is an island, Anglesey is an island, and Llyn Cerrig Bach may itself have contained an island sanctuary in ancient times. Perhaps this triple symbolism was spiritually significant.

Evidence of waterside rituals in Europe predates the Iron Age, but very many sites date from the La Tène period – including La Tène itself. In Iron Age Britain the River Thames and the River Witham in Lincolnshire attracted precious votive offerings such as ceremonial shields and helmets, swords and spears.

At Lindow Moss in Cheshire, a wetland area about 180 kilometres (110 miles) east of Llyn Cerrig Bach, there is compelling evidence of human sacrifice. They include the remains of a 25 year old man. Although he died at some point between 2 BC and AD 119, his body was preserved like leather in the cold, acidic, deoxygenated water of a peat bog. He wore a fox-fur armband. His last meal had been a bannock of wheat and barley, and his gut also contained mistletoe pollen. He had suffered a triple killing – axe blows to the head, strangulation by a cord and cutting of the throat. This suggests a ritual killing, perhaps by Druids.

It is quite possible that the Anglesey wetlands too were places of human sacrifice, but none of the bones held in the Amgueddfa Cymru – National Museum Wales collection are of human origin.

Ritual killings also took place in wetlands during the Iron Age. This body was recovered from Lindow Moss in 1984.

LAKES ARE OFTEN BELIEVED TO BE THE HOME OF GODS OR GODDESSES, WATER SPIRITS OR MONSTERS

Ritual sites & sanctuaries

Was Llyn Cerrig Bach a sanctuary, dedicated to a god of war?
Miranda Aldhouse-Green *compares Llyn Cerrig Bach to similar sites in Britain and Gaul*

Archaeological evidence from Llyn Cerrig Bach suggests that the lake attracted repeated ritual activity, from at least the fourth century BC to the second century AD. The site may well have been a highly revered shrine, drawing pilgrims from some distance.

The absence of contemporary texts means that we cannot link this wetland sanctuary to any specific cult or deity. We are dependent upon the surviving artefacts to give the site its voice; any meaningful interpretation has to carry an element of speculation. Two aspects of Llyn Cerrig Bach stand out: its watery nature and the prestigious – often martial – character of the 'offerings', including the two iron slave-gang chains.

It has long been generally accepted that built sanctuaries were less important to Iron Age communities than natural features in the landscape, such as rivers, trees, mountains, springs and lakes. To an extent that view still holds good, but a steadily increasing body of evidence suggests that such natural features could be modified by people and that sometimes shrines were constructed.

Llyn Cerrig Bach itself may have had a wooden bridge or causeway to a central island. This tradition can be traced in other prehistoric watery depositional sites as far apart as Flag Fen in Cambridgeshire, Fiskerton in Lincolnshire and the iconic offering-place at La Tène, on the edge of Lake Neuchâtel in Switzerland. All of these watery sites have in common the deposition of high-status objects, including weaponry. Most of them contain human remains that could have been sacrificial victims, maybe prisoners of war.

A group of built shrines in northern Gaul dates from the middle Iron Age. These have certain features that chime with the evidence from Llyn Cerrig Bach, and are known as 'war sanctuaries'. The most notable of them, dated to the fourth century BC, is at the French village of Gournay-sur-Aronde. This site was carefully situated at the boundary between at least three tribal territories. A rectangular wooden building was erected around a central pit, in which the remains of sacrificed oxen were placed until the flesh had rotted. The bones were then carefully and strategically placed in the enclosure ditch surrounding the shrine, along with the complete bodies of horses and human remains. Trophy-armour belonging to prisoners of war was displayed within the temple, and it seems likely that Gournay was dedicated to a war deity.

Caesar describes such a god as having heaps of war booty, including weapons and armour, offered to him in thanks for victory in battle:

> "… they sacrifice whatever captured animals may have survived the conflict, and collect the other things into one place. In many states you may see piles of these things heaped up in their consecrated spots; nor does it often happen that any one … dares either to secrete in his house things captured, or take away those deposited; and the most severe punishment, with torture, has been established for such a deed."
>
> *Julius Caesar* The Gallic War XI,17

In Britain, we may point to similar, though later, sanctuaries, such as Hayling Island in Hampshire, where in about 50 BC, a wooden circular shrine was erected. Ritual deposits, including weaponry and the sacrificial remains of animals, were made in its courtyard. The martial equipment and the remains of what may have been war-carts found at Llyn Cerrig Bach have resonance with these built war-shrines. The slave-chains may likewise reflect booty in the form of prisoners-of-war. Gournay, Hayling Island and Llyn Cerrig Bach all have in common the habitual ritual destruction of metal objects, particularly swords.

The study of similar sites in Britain and Ireland, and across the Channel in Gaul, demonstrates that Llyn Cerrig Bach formed part of a network of holy sites centred on special places in the landscape. The position of Llyn Cerrig Bach, like Hayling, on an offshore island, is likely to have been significant. There is considerable evidence to suggest that islands were charged with spiritual meaning in the Iron Age. Islands, like marshes and pools, were edgy places, meeting points between the divine and the mundane worlds. It is possible to imagine that the whole Isle of Anglesey, not just the watery shrine itself, had spiritual significance.

Miranda Aldhouse-Green
is Professor of Archaeology
at Cardiff University

Islands such as Anglesey and waterside locations such as Llyn Cerrig Bach seem to have had important spiritual connotations throughout Iron Age Europe

AD60: A reckoning with Rome

"[Suetonius Paulinus] prepared accordingly to attack the island of Mona [Anglesey], which had a considerable population of its own, while serving as a haven for refugees; and, in view of the shallow and variable channel, constructed a flotilla of boats with flat bottoms. By this method the infantry crossed; the cavalry, who followed, did so by fording or, in deeper water, by swimming at the side of their horses.

"On the beach stood the adverse array, a serried mass of arms and men, with women flitting between the ranks. In the style of Furies, in robes of deathly black and with dishevelled hair, they brandished their torches; while a circle of Druids, lifting their hands to heaven and showering imprecations, struck the troops with such awe at the extraordinary spectacle that, as though their limbs were paralysed, they exposed their bodies to wounds without an attempt at movement.

"Then, reassured by their general, and inciting each other never to flinch before a band of females and fanatics, they charged behind the standards, cut down all who met them, and enveloped the enemy in his own flames."

Tacitus, *Annals* XIV, 29-30

THE END OF AN ERA

During the first century BC and the first century AD the Roman empire expanded relentlessly northwards. The Britons had their first taste of the legions in 55 and 54 BC, when Julius Caesar crossed the channel to attack the tribes of the southeast. The occupation of Britain began in AD 43, during the reign of the emperor Claudius, but it would take the legions over three decades of campaigning in the west and north, from AD 47 onwards, to secure the conquest.

Resistance by the British tribes was fierce. An initial leader of the native resistance was Caratacus (known in Wales as Caradoc), a leader of the Catuvellauni who had conquered the territory of the Atrebates in the AD 40s. In the face of the Roman onslaught he retreated westwards, fighting against the Romans with the Silures of south Wales and then further north with the Ordovices. Defeated in AD 51, he escaped to the tribal lands of the Brigantes (modern Yorkshire), where he was betrayed by Queen Cartimandua and handed over to the Romans. Taken in chains to Rome, his passionate defence of his actions so impressed the emperor Claudius that he was pardoned and lived the rest of his days in Italy.

Anglesey was first taken in AD 60, but the Roman troops had to be recalled to subdue Boudicca's rebellion in eastern and southern Britain. Anglesey was reconquered by the general Gaius Julius Agricola in AD 78. The Caledonian tribes were defeated in AD 84, but northern Scotland was never overcome, and Ireland too remained unconquered. Llyn Cerrig Bach therefore found itself on the very northwestern edge of the mighty Roman empire. Linked by a new network of roads, the military maintained Roman rule across the western and northern frontier zones of Britain. Many of the troops were auxiliaries, support units recruited from all over the empire.

The Celtic culture of Iron Age Britain did not come to an abrupt end with the arrival of the Romans. Even as the legions advanced, fine artefacts in the La Tène style were still being produced. A mixed or hybrid culture that is known as Romano-British gradually developed. In southern Britain, and later in parts of the west and north, the Roman way of life became well

The settlement at Din Lligwy, near Moelfre, survived into the Romano-British period. Finds have included Roman coins, a silver ingot, glassware and pottery.

established, with the building of luxurious villas with great estates. In more remote frontier areas, native farms supplied the legionary forts with grain, hides and other goods. In much of Wales, farmsteads such as Din Lligwy remained occupied in much the same way as they had been during the Iron Age.

The power of the Druids was broken, but Celtic deities were often merged with Roman equivalents. Sulis, goddess of the springs at Bath, was identified with Minerva. In the countryside, springs and wells were still sacred and no doubt ancient shrines were still visited in the woods. Christianity, legalised in AD 313, rapidly spread amongst Romans and Britons.

We now know that the use of Llyn Cerrig Bach as a shrine extended for perhaps 50 or 100 years into this Romano-British era. At some point during the second century AD the offerings were no longer being made on Anglesey. As the centuries passed, the lakes and fens kept their secret.

THE OLD SPIRITUAL WORLD TYPIFIED BY LLYN CERRIG BACH WAS SLIPPING AWAY INTO THE MISTS AND SHADOWS

4

SUNKEN TREASURE

DECORATIVE BRONZE

Whenever the Llyn Cerrig Bach treasure is on display, it is a crescent-shaped piece of copper alloy that first catches the eye. It has a dull gleam. It reminded Sir Cyril Fox of the ceremonial ornaments known as *lunulae* ('small moons'), which were made in Britain, Ireland and France between about 2200 and 1900 BC. At first glance one might think this crescent, too, was a decorative collar, but its central hole is too small even for the neck of a child.

Closer examination shows small holes, clearly designed for fixing onto a surface. This artefact is therefore catalogued as a 'crescentic plaque'. All sorts of possibilities for its original use have been considered, such as a collar for a cult statue, a decoration for a shield, the flared end-piece of a trumpet or an embellishment for a war chariot: the size of the central hole might have fitted nicely around the base of the central pole. However we cannot be certain.

The plaque is a thin sheet of metal that has been hammered from behind to create a raised pattern, a technique known as repoussé. Larger holes once held studs. The broadest section of the metal is decorated with a triple-lobed motif known as a triskele. This derives from the word for 'three-legged' in Ancient Greek; the Welsh is *trisgel*.

The triple spiral is a very ancient symbol, being carved as early as 3200 BC on the Newgrange megalithic tomb in Ireland. During the Iron Age the more angular triskele became used in decorative metalwork, and this example from Llyn Cerrig Bach is in the later artistic tradition of Insular La Tène, perhaps being made in about 100 BC. The central roundel has a lively asymmetrical triskele worked in two planes of repoussé relief and flanked by an arrangement of triple fleshy leaves. It clearly reveals a fascination with groups of three (triads), and is judged to represent a significant moment in the development of the native triskele designs.

Six thin plaques of copper alloy were also found at Llyn Cerrig Bach. They are thought to be 'casket ornaments', but they too may well have adorned the sides of a chariot. They include squares, rectangular strips and a triple roundel or tri-disc. The scrolled designs are of a later date than those on the crescentic plaque, possibly from after the Roman conquest, and are of less artistic merit. The repeated symmetrical patterns have been punched with a die.

Nine other strips or ribbons of copper alloy have been found. They are coiled in spirals and some have later been folded flat. They could possibly have been wrapped around a wooden staff or some ceremonial regalia.

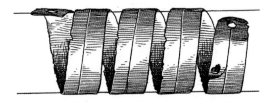

A CRESCENT OF BRONZE, PATTERNED IN STYLE
... BUT WHAT COULD IT HAVE BEEN USED FOR?

HARNESSES & WHEELS

The depths of Llyn Cerrig Bach received many treasures associated with horses. Many parts remain from harnesses and from chariots or carts. They include some fine pieces of metalwork. A leap of imagination, based upon the available archaeological research, can be used to put together a picture of an Iron Age warrior poised in full battle array, his charioteer crouching forward with the reins as they hurtle through the gates of a hillfort. The chariot lurches and bounces; the hooves of two wiry little horses kick up a storm of dust. Julius Caesar himself marvelled at the Britons' ability to ride over steep and dangerous slopes (*The Gallic War* IV, 33).

*Chariot burials, such as that at Garton Slack, York (**above**) confirm the importance of chariots and horses from the Middle Iron Age onwards. So too does the votive offering of chariots and harnesses at Llyn Cerrig Bach.*

The treasure includes perhaps 11 to 16 bridle bits, either made of bronze or of iron plated with bronze. Bits are the metal pieces held in the horse's mouth, and are attached by rings to the reins. They are used to guide the horse. There are several different designs in the assemblage, with the bit made of either two or three links in addition to the tubular rein-rings. One bit has a single curved bar. One of the Llyn Cerrig Bach bits is Irish, the rest are British. All date from the later Iron Age, but their precise age is unclear.

Bridle bit

Only three terrets were found at Llyn Cerrig Bach, each from a different chariot and each with signs of having been used. They are cast from bronze, but one has an iron fitting. Terrets, quite a common find in Britain, are oval rings designed to hold the reins and prevent them from tangling, and four or five were fitted to the top of the wooden yoke.

The ends of the wooden yoke turned upwards and may have been capped by finials. That is one possible explanation for the function of the bronze 'horn cap' found at Llyn Cerrig Bach. This forms a decorative waisted cylinder with a separate disc sealing one end. The disc has been rather crudely punched with fine dots in the shape of a swastika, a cross with bent arms. In this version of the motif, the right angles of the main cross have been blocked in with squares enclosing diagonal crosses. The swastika was already a sacred symbol in Asia for millennia before the Iron Age. Twenty-seven similar swastikas adorn the famous Battersea shield.

Horn cap

The draught pole of an Iron Age chariot was also made of wood – a fragment found at Llyn Cerrig Bach was of oak partly bound with iron (*see* p.69).

Chariot wheels were spoked and wooden, between about 75 and 120 centimetres in diameter, with most measuring about 90 centimetres. At Llyn Cerrig Bach the wood was rotted away, leaving only the iron tyres, nave-hoops and linch-pins. Most tyres were in broken sections. One was made of fine quality steel, but others are of cruder iron and may have belonged to simple carts.

Wheels were attached to the axle by removable pegs called linch-pins. Of the two examples found at Llyn Cerrig Bach, one was made of iron and was topped with a ring. The other was made of bronze and iron and had a more decorative head.

The wooden hubs of chariot wheels

Nave hoop

are known as naves. They were lathe-turned and were strengthened against splitting by a nave hoop. Eight hoops were found at Llyn Cerrig Bach: four in iron and four more decorative ones in bronze. Three more iron hoops were later found west of the lake. Their date is more uncertain.

How many chariots or other vehicles were sent spinning into the dark waters of Llyn Cerrig Bach? It is impossible to say. Parts of at least 23 iron tyres have been recovered, but it is always possible that individual detached wheels were offered to the gods, as precious or possibly sacred objects in their own right. Wheel motifs often represent sun-gods.

THE TREASURED POSSESSIONS OF CHARIOTEERS — BRIDLE BITS FOR THE HORSES, IRON TYRES FOR THE WOODEN WHEELS

Chariots ride again

Can we reconstruct the appearance of a complete Iron Age chariot?
Frances Lynch picks over the available evidence

Horses have been a symbol of status and power ever since the Late Bronze Age.

In Early Iron Age Europe a royal burial might include a fine wagon and sometimes the sacrificed horses, too. By the fifth century BC the preferred vehicle was a two-wheeled carriage or chariot, with the body laid out on a board across its floor.

From the third century BC we have about 20 chariot burials (of both men and women) found near Garton (*see* p50) and Wetwang in the East Riding of Yorkshire. In contrast to continental practice these chariots were normally dismantled, the wheels removed and placed at the side of the grave or laid over the pole. The body was placed in a sleeping position within the chariot, often with a sword and in one case a suit of chain mail,

and always with a joint of pork for the journey to the next life. Llyn Cerrig Bach is the only British chariot find which is not a burial.

A Llyn Cerrig Bach chariot was reconstructed by Sir Cyril Fox in 1946. He began on paper and then produced a small-scale model for the National Museum of Wales. Finally he created a much larger model for the Festival of Britain in 1951. Fox had only the limited material evidence outlined on page 50. One leg-bone of a horse indicated its size, just 11 hands (112 centimetres from the ground to the withers). To this primary evidence Fox added images of chariots from coins, gravestones and wall paintings, most of them admittedly Mediterranean examples. He also studied accounts of war chariots in the work of Roman writers. Fox's reconstruction (*below*)

has remained one of the most influential images of the British Iron Age and the baseline against which other interpretations have been measured. However his original proposals may need some modification in the light of more recent finds.

Fox's reconstruction of the wheels has stood the test of time, but his suggestion of a swingle-tree (a harness crossbar) has not been accepted. Details of the yoke remain uncertain. Yoking horses is not the most effective way of using their traction power, but this was the method used until the adoption of the horse collar in the ninth century AD. The yoke position, forward of the withers or behind, is crucial to the angle of the pole and to the position of the carriage body in relation to the axle. The forward position is better, but stresses the horses. Perhaps this did not matter to the Iron Age warrior.

Modern detective work can reveal more information about the vanished woodwork of chariots. The method of discovery is to pour latex into the voids created by the decay of the wood. In this way the length of the axle (usually about two metres) and the pole (normally three metres), have

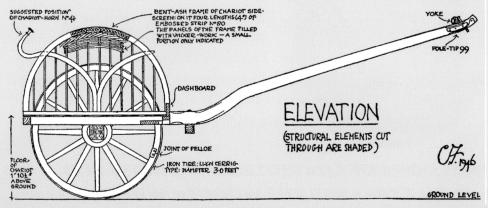

SUGGESTED POSITION OF CHARIOT-HORN Nº 4

BENT-ASH FRAME OF CHARIOT SIDE-SCREEN: ON IT FOUR LENGTHS (4.7) OF EMBOSSED STRIP Nº 50 THE PANELS OF THE FRAME FILLED WITH VICKER-WORK — A SMALL PORTION ONLY INDICATED

YOKE

POLE-TIP 99

DASHBOARD

FLOOR OF CHARIOT 1'10½" ABOVE GROUND

JOINT OF FELLOE

IRON TIRE: LLYN CERRIG TYPE: DIAMETER 3.0 FEET

ELEVATION

(STRUCTURAL ELEMENTS CUT THROUGH ARE SHADED)

CF 1946

GROUND LEVEL

been quite satisfactorily established. The 12-spoked wheels have diameters of 90-100cm.

Debate still surrounds the size, shape and position of the lightweight carriage body, and how it was attached to the more substantial frame. Since these vehicles could be readily dismantled, it is possible that bodies were interchangeable. Perhaps they could be adapted to serve as a closed travelling carriage, an open fighting platform or even as a bier or coffin. The evidence from the British sites is variable.

Suspension is another issue. Fox suggested a planked floor, although this would have provided a very bumpy ride. Most theories have favoured a floor woven from strips of rawhide, to absorb some of the jolts. One recent reconstruction is based upon Y-shaped struts visible on a chariot which feature on a Gaulish coin. This proposal suggests that the floor was a separate platform within the body framework, suspended by four rawhide straps from its double arched sides. Experiment has shown that this worked well, but it also showed that an experienced charioteer could manage to stay upright even on a hard planked floor.

Frances Lynch is an Honorary Research Fellow of Bangor University

WEAPONS OF WAR

The seven iron spearheads or fragments from Llyn Cerrig Bach are wicked looking weapons reinforced by a central ridge, typical of the La Tène style across Europe. One was socketed to a shaft of ash. One spearhead has an extreme length, at 72 centimetres. This suggests that some spears may have been designed chiefly to impress, perhaps used in some ceremony or ritual.

The Llyn Cerrig Bach peat yielded up the remains of eleven iron swords, sword fittings and mountings of iron or copper alloy. They probably vary greatly in their dates, and some may be among the earliest votive offerings at this site. Like other items of the assemblage, several weapons, such as the two swords on page 66, have been deliberately damaged or folded in ancient times, probably for ritual reasons

The swords are all two-edged, but vary in their dimensions. Two swords have narrow blades between 36 and 38 millimetres wide, and are still sheathed in remains of iron scabbards. Another group has broader blades of between 43 and 56 millimetres. Two sword blades have survived at their full lengths, namely 69 and 76 centimetres. The other blades are only partial, but some of the broader ones must originally have been 90 centimetres or longer. On page 17 Mary Davis of National Museum Wales draws attention to two small symbols stamped on blades during manufacture. We cannot know if these were marks of quality, maker's marks or talismans.

The swords are all of a style associated with southern Britain. Whether they were captured in battle, acquired by trade or brought to Anglesey by refugees or pilgrims is unknown. Insufficient is known about sword manufacture in what is now north Wales to offer detailed comparisons. The upper half of an iron dagger, similar to some found in Somerset, is also part of the assemblage.

*Many of the offerings left at Llyn Cerrig Bach are associated with warfare, such as the iron spearheads (**left**), the swords (**shown on pages 24 and 66**) and the bronze mounting for a shield boss (**opposite, and page 74**)*

Shields were about a metre in height, and made of wood and leather. As these are perishable, only the metal parts of shields generally survive. From Llyn Cerrig Bach there remains a convex shield mounting, hammered from bronze, which would have covered the central boss. The mount's elegant vertical extensions, ending in fishtail shapes, would have covered the shield's strengthening rib. Fox reports that the mounting was originally found in a 'crumpled condition', but was restored in the laboratory of the British Museum. This suggests that it was already detached from the wooden shield when it was thrown into the lake. Shields were often dedicated to the gods as votive offerings, even in token form as miniatures.

The fine, swirling lines of its decoration are perhaps viewed most clearly when transcribed onto a page. That they were originally engraved freehand on a curved bronze sheet was an amazing feat. The powerful triskele motif, probably seen as a protective charm, appears here in four asymmetrical patterns. These writhe with energy and life, possibly putting a modern viewer in mind of the circle dance paintings by Henri Matisse. Ancient comparisons relate to the intricate decoration found on Insular La Tène hand mirrors. The boss mounting is surely the most splendid item in the Llyn Cerrig Bach assemblage. The date for this shield would probably have been at some time in the first century BC or the first century AD.

Two small crescents of bronze are also part of the assemblage, and it has been suggested that these mountings may have flanked a shield-boss, although probably not this one. The Llyn Cerrig Bach shield might once have had larger flanking decorations, as have been found on discoveries at other sites in north Wales. Shield parts found in 1872 at Moel Hiraddug, near Dyserth, include a flanking plaque in the crescentic pelta shape. A discovery in 1963 on the slopes of Cader Idris near Tal-y-Llyn included a shield-boss with a repoussé triskele. It is possible that these shields represent a regional style of north Wales.

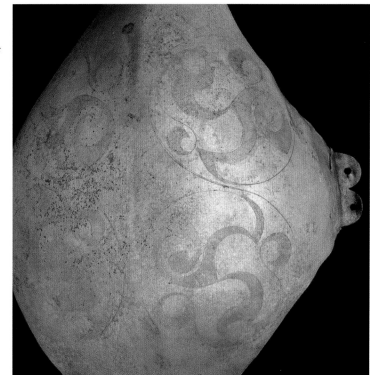
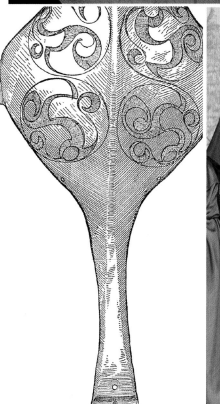

SWORDS, SCABBARDS, SPEARS, SHIELDS ... ULTIMATE STATUS SYMBOLS FOR THE WARRIOR ELITE

(above) Shackled: a single chain was passed through the neck pieces.

(below) A relief from Mogontiacum (Roman Mainz, in Germany) shows two captives chained by the neck.

GANG CHAINS

Because of the remarkable story of their discovery, the gang chains remain the most famous artefacts from Llyn Cerrig Bach. There are two of these, both made of wrought iron. The first is complete, with five hinged neck pieces joined by figure-of-eight shaped links. The total length of the chain is about three metres; it weighs 6·6 kilograms. The prisoners would have been held about 60 centimetres apart. The second chain is of a similar design, but is smaller, broken and missing a link and a section of chain.

Shackles were a common sight in the ancient world. Slavery was a fact of life in most Iron Age societies and the Roman empire could not have survived without a slave class, which at one time may have made up over one-sixth of the whole imperial population. Many captured prisoners of war and defeated communities were sold into slavery. Shackles were a powerful symbol of subjugation, and no Roman emperor's 'triumph' (victory parade) was complete without defeated leaders of the enemy being displayed in chains.

Writing before the Roman conquest, Strabo lists slaves – along with metals, cattle, hides, hunting dogs and grain – as Britain's best known exports. It could be that his comments referred to a particular period, perhaps when the southern and eastern British tribes were supplying slaves to the Roman occupiers of Gaul. It is not clear how prevalent slavery was elsewhere in Britain. There are no finds of gang chains outside the southeast except Llyn Cerrig Bach, which suggests that they may well have arrived in Anglesey from that area.

The chains of Llyn Cerrig Bach may also have been used in punishing criminals, in securing prisoners of war, or in forced labour, but this particular location would suggest that they carried greater ritual significance. They could have been symbols of power or of victory in battle. They might be dated between the mid first century BC and the first century AD. They could have been used by Romans before or during the conquest, to enslave British captives. If the chains had later been seized from the Romans during an ambush, throwing them into the sacred lake might have been a symbolic act of defiance.

WERE THESE CHAINS USED TO HUMILIATE
WARRIORS CAPTURED IN BATTLE ?

Sounding out : a reconstruction of the trumpa from Loughnashade, played here by Simon O'Dwyer

A BRONZE HORN

Amongst the most intriguing finds at Llyn Cerrig Bach were the remains of a large, curved horn. Might this very instrument once have provided the 'soundtrack' to ancient lakeside rituals?

It may have been made between the second century BC and the first century AD, possibly in Britain or possibly in Ireland. Its original length may have been over 180 centimetres. All that survives is a 35·7 centimetre tubular fragment attached to a prominent central knob of cast bronze; the latter covered a joint between the two main sections. The diameter is 27 millimetres. The seam of the copper alloy tube is riveted on alternate sides to an inner strip. The horn was patched in ancient times, presumably to remedy an air leak, but there is debate as to whether this was carried out by the original manufacturer or later, as a running repair. When discovered, the horn section was found squashed and twisted, but was restored to its original shape.

Ancient types of war horn included the curved Roman *cornu*, which sounded the charge or the retreat of troops in battle, and the long, upright carnyx of the Celtic lands. The bell of the latter was shaped like a snarling animal and it produced eerie yelping and droning sounds.

The Llyn Cerrig Bach horn belongs to a different group of musical instruments, with varied designs. All of them are riveted, suggesting that lead and silver soldering was not used at the time of their manufacture in the Late Iron Age. They are generally known by the Irish name *trumpa*. Only five survive in Europe. One is from Llyn Cerrig Bach. Four are from Ireland, of which two are complete and one is even playable. A further contender was found in France, but this one is not riveted and may not be authentic. The bell of the Loughnashade horn, found in a lake near the ancient site of Eamhain Macha in County Armagh, is richly decorated with late La Tène motifs. Further Irish examples were discovered in the nineteenth century, but have since been lost.

It is uncertain how these big horns were held to be played. Similar curved horns are known today in northern India and Nepal.

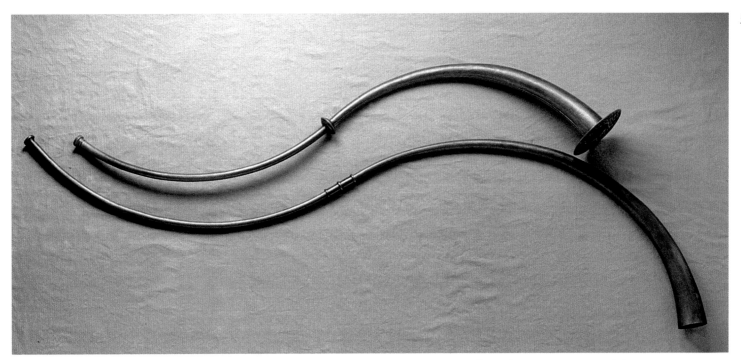

Were these also war horns? The musician Simon O'Dwyer, an expert in the instruments of Irish prehistory, points out the very accurate intervals of these horns, suggesting that their use was musical as well as martial. He points out that the Middle Irish saga *Táin bó Fraích*, which describes the engagement of Fraích to Findabair, daughter of Queen Medb, includes elements deriving from the first century BC. In it, seven horn players are described as producing music of great beauty with healing powers. This would suggest that the Llyn Cerrig Bach horn might have been used in religious or betrothal ceremonies and also on the battlefield.

(above) Reconstructions of the sinuous Loughnashade and Ard Brinn horns.
(right and below) The restored fragment of the Llyn Cerrig Bach horn.

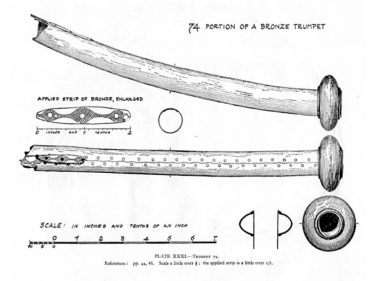

74 PORTION OF A BRONZE TRUMPET

APPLIED STRIP OF BRONZE, ENLARGED

SCALE: IN INCHES AND TENTHS OF AN INCH

PLATE XXXI—Trumpet 74.
References: pp. 44, 86. Scale a little over ⅓; the applied strip is a little over 1/1.

IMAGINE THE EERIE SOUND OF THE HORNS BOOMING THROUGH A MISTY DAWN AT LLYN CERRIG BACH

(left) Pair of blacksmith's long tongs.

(below) Short gripping tongs.

In 2012, during examination in preparation for making a replica, Celtic art decoration was discovered on the short tongs by David Chapman and National Museum staff.

Overlaid drawing
(Tony Daly)

IRON WORK

Iron and metalworking played an important part in the mythology of Iron Age Europe. Hephaistos was blacksmith to the gods of Ancient Greece, and Vulcan was his counterpart in Ancient Rome. The master smith Völundr or Wayland appears in Germanic mythology. Celtic myths refer to a smith god known as Gofannon in Welsh and Giobhniu in Irish. Traditions associated with iron would later continue in the folklore, fairy tales and superstitions of Christian Europe. That could be why people still nail up an iron horseshoe above a door to bring good luck.

Five file-shaped iron bars (two of them whole and three of them partial) were recovered out of the peat from Llyn Cerrig Bach. Many iron bars like these have been found in the British Isles. They vary in weight and design.

They have in the past been categorised as 'currency bars', used for payment, but in fact their use may have been very different from that of coins (which were first minted in Britain by the Britons of the southeast in the second century BC). The debate about the bars' use has also previously included speculation that some were 'bar shares', used in ploughing, or perhaps just representing the iron-shod plough as symbols of agriculture and fertility. It was suggested that others may have had a purely ritual significance in their own right. Today's explanation (overleaf), put forward by Peter and Susan Crew, is more convincing. They regard the bars as a convenient form of exchanging metal that would later be used in a forge. This explanation may be more prosaic, but even as votive offerings these bars would still represent wealth, power and the blacksmith's magical skills.

Two pairs of tongs are part of the Llyn Cerrig Bach treasure, both being practical working tools. The longer one, at over 53 centimetres, was designed to hold red hot iron while it was being hammered on the anvil. The shorter one, at about 20 centimetres, might have been used to grip a bronze sheet for riveting. Other iron artefacts include a pliable knife. The presence of these tools might be explained by the high status of the smith, by the honouring of a god associated with metalworking, or perhaps by a local population continuing to make offerings at the site after the Roman conquest and the decline of the warrior elite.

An artist's reconstruction of a smithy in one of the rectangular workshops at the Romano-British settlement, Din Lligwy. (Also see the illustration on page 45)

A fragment of an iron blade may belong to a scythe, but a well preserved whole blade (with a tang to support a handle) belongs to a sickle. It is of the 'balanced' type still common today, in which the blade forms an extreme curve which bends back from the handle. It may have been used for thatching or for the harvest. This type of sickle first appears during the La Tène period. Its presence at a ritual site may be connected with harvest rituals. In the ancient world food and agricultural implements were powerful symbols of fertility and regeneration. The Roman writer Pliny the Elder, writing in about AD 77, describes a sacrificial ritual in Gaul at which Druids, dressed in white robes, use a golden sickle to cut mistletoe from an oak tree. (*see* p.25)

TO THE CELTS IRON WAS HELD IN AWE, SIGNIFYING POWER AND PRESTIGE. EVERY CHIEFTAIN'S HOUSEHOLD HAD ITS OWN SMITHY

Bars & blacksmiths

What exactly were 'currency bars' and what can they reveal about the Iron Age?
Peter and Susan Crew discuss the importance and value of early iron

It is now generally accepted that so-called currency bars, like those found at Llyn Cerrig Bach, were not used for monetary exchange. They were a form of trade iron, with the different types being the products of individual or regional workshops using different types of iron ore. The distinctive shapes of the bars are like trade marks showing both the source of the iron, its quality and its working properties. The consistency of the weights of each type of bar is a result of well established and frequently repeated cycles of smelting, refining and smithing.

More than 1,500 currency bars are now known from Britain, mainly from central southern areas, with over ninety percent being found in hoards containing 100 bars or more. There are at least 20 distinctive types, which can be distinguished by their shape, dimensions and the form of their sockets and tips.

To make a currency bar it is necessary to refine and weld a raw bloom (a spongy mixture of iron and slag) into compact iron. This can then be drawn down to a thin bar, with one end being splayed and bent to form a socket. Occasionally the other end is folded back on itself and welded.

These are all basic blacksmithing operations and the final form of the bar is a demonstration of the quality of the iron and its suitability for forging into objects.

The five examples of iron bars from Llyn Cerrig Bach are of two types. The first type is represented by a slight and very well forged bar, with a small tubular socket. The other four bars are rather heavier, with shallow sockets made by raising the edges of the bar. All the bars are in a remarkably good state of preservation, with little corrosion and still retaining much of their original surfaces.

It is likely that the two types of bar found at Llyn Cerrig Bach were made at different places. The one with the tubular socket is very similar in shape and weight to those found in large hoards near Malvern. The other heavier bars with shallow sockets are, so far, unique to Llyn Cerrig Bach and may well be a more local product, though this remains to be demonstrated by metallurgical and slag inclusion analysis.

One superficially insignificant piece of iron found at Llyn Cerrig Bach is in fact a fragment of a very well forged rectangular bar from which the ends have been cut. This is exactly the type of partly-used stock which can be found in any blacksmith's workshop. Along with the tongs, the currency bars and the fragmentary and often worn tyres, this suggests that a significant proportion of the hoard might have derived from a smith's stock in trade. This raises the intriguing possibility that a large number of the objects from Llyn Cerrig Bach were not ritual offerings, but were carefully hidden, in troubled times, in a place from which subsequent recovery would not be difficult.

Experimental iron working has demonstrated the considerable value of prehistoric iron. To make one kilogram of fully refined bar iron required about 100 kilograms of charcoal and a total of 25 man-day's work. To make all the iron objects in the hoard would have required some 250 kilograms of bar iron or 500 kilograms of bloom (because of the considerable losses in refining and smithing). This is equivalent to about half of the total production from Crawcwellt, in Merioneth, one of the largest prehistoric iron-working sites yet known in Britain. This is a clear indication both of the value of the iron in the Llyn Cerrig Bach hoard and of the importance of iron in the later prehistoric economy.

Peter and Susan Crew worked as archaeologists for the Snowdonia National Park until 2007

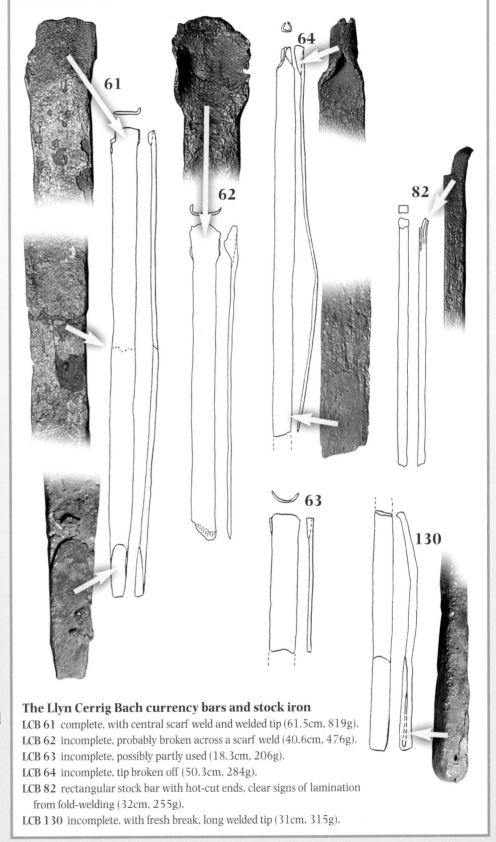

The Llyn Cerrig Bach currency bars and stock iron

LCB 61 complete, with central scarf weld and welded tip (61.5cm, 819g).

LCB 62 incomplete, probably broken across a scarf weld (40.6cm, 476g).

LCB 63 incomplete, possibly partly used (18.3cm, 206g).

LCB 64 incomplete, tip broken off (50.3cm, 284g).

LCB 82 rectangular stock bar with hot-cut ends, clear signs of lamination from fold-welding (32cm, 255g).

LCB 130 incomplete, with fresh break, long welded tip (31cm, 315g).

(above) Cauldrons were everyday cooking utensils, suspended over the hearth.

(below) This image on the Gundestrup cauldron suggests a powerful symbolic or ritual role, associated with sacrifice and rebirth.

THE CAULDRONS

Some of the copper alloy fragments in Llyn Cerrig Bach belonged to cauldrons. Originally it was believed that there were two of these, but it is now thought that at least three or four may have been left in the lake. These examples are without embellishments. They are missing their rims and handles and seem to have been repeatedly patched. They could date from the first century BC to the early years of the second century AD.

The cauldrons may have been damaged on purpose, like many other artefacts from the lake. If so, this might suggest that they were intentional offerings rather than abandoned pots and pans. The cauldron was at the centre of communal hearths, the bringer of sustenance in hungry times, the provider of lavish feasts for the chieftain's household and family in times of plenty. A cauldron therefore could be seen as a symbol of hospitality and generosity, or perhaps as a funeral gift which would be of practical use in the next life.

It was a long-lasting symbol, as other Welsh finds demonstrate. Two cauldrons of Bronze Age type were found in 1913 with other very early iron objects at Llyn Fawr, a lake in the northern Cynon valley, south Wales: a cauldron from the late first to second century AD was found at Manorbier, Pembrokeshire, containing equipment for wine drinking, and one dating from about 120 AD was buried in a rich grave at Welshpool.

Large cauldrons would have been used in ceremonies and might be associated with ritual feasts, sacrifice, potions or libations. A splendid silver cauldron was found at Gundestrup, Denmark. It was possibly made in Thrace, yet has motifs and scenes typical of the La Tène cultural world. It is decorated with humans and animals, an antlered figure (perhaps the god known as Cernunnos, holding a torc, *see* p.38), warriors, the killing of a bull, and a warrior being dropped head first into a cauldron.

The latter image resonates with a story from the *Mabinogi*, the Welsh tales written down in the Middle Ages which retain so many insights into the pre-Christian world. Bendigeidfran, King of Britain, is at war in Ireland. The Irish light a fire under the Cauldron of Rebirth and throw into it their dead warriors, who are then regenerated to fight again. The king's half-brother

Efnysien pretends to be a dead Irishman. When he is thrown into the cauldron, he stretches his body so that the cauldron breaks into four pieces but his own heart breaks too, for the victory of the Britons has come at such a heavy cost.

(**below left**) *A fragment from the Llyn Cerrig Bach cauldrons.*

(**below right**) *A much earlier cauldron, dating from about 800-600 BC, was recovered from Llyn Fawr, a lake in south Wales.*

It has even been suggested that the Celtic 'cauldron of rebirth' is a prototype for the 'grail' legends of medieval Europe, in which a sacred vessel offers spiritual rebirth in the Christian sense. In folklore and popular culture, cauldrons are still associated with magic, witchcraft and wizardry.

CAULDRONS WERE ASSOCIATED WITH DAILY SUSTENANCE AND WITH THE HOSPITALITY OF A NOBLE HOUSEHOLD. WERE THEY ALSO RITUAL VESSELS, LINKED WITH MYTHS OF REBIRTH?

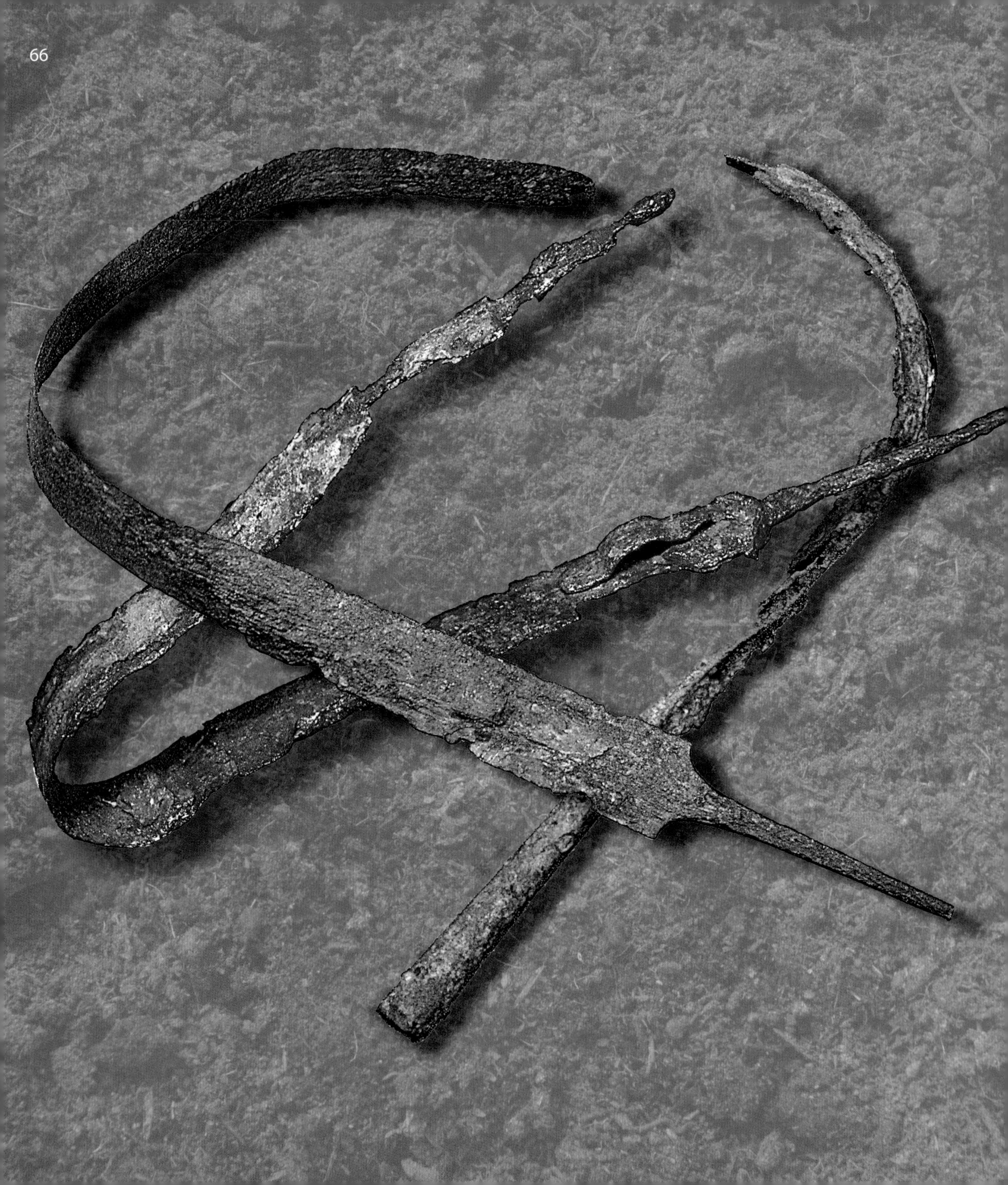

5 RIDDLES OF THE LAKE

LIKE MANY ARCHAEOLOGICAL SITES, Llyn Cerrig Bach remains an enigma. What secrets does it hold? If we take stock of the material evidence, as well as research carried out into the nature of Iron Age societies, what conclusions can we reach?

Several theories have been put forward as to how the assemblage was deposited. Sir Cyril Fox was the first to consider the artefacts to be votive offerings. Since then, some voices have been raised which are more sceptical about the ritual nature of the site. The maritime historian Owain T. P. Roberts has argued that the Llyn Cerrig Bach area could once have been part of the coast and that these artefacts represent a shipwrecked Iron Age cargo. This view has been contradicted by the geophysical surveys of Philip Macdonald. Peter and Susan Crew (see p.62) consider the possibility that at least some of the artefacts might have been part of a blacksmith's hoard. Even so, the ritual theory has remained the most commonly held view amongst archaeologists. Why?

The artefacts mostly represent status, power or wealth. They include many military items, but none which would indicate domestic occupation of the site during the Iron Age, such as jewellery, querns or spindle whorls. There is no evidence of a midden or of the foundations of roundhouses. Indeed, the location may have been chosen for its remote situation. We do not know if the swords, spears and shield mounting were precious personal possessions or the booty of war.

(left) These two swords and a spearhead from Llyn Cerrig Bach have been deliberately bent and folded over, and so rendered powerless

The deliberate spoiling of many of the artefacts is a common feature of votive offerings, representing perhaps a desire to render them powerless, to destroy their magic. As we have learned, the finding of so many animal bones suggests that sacrifice was another form of offering at this site, as at many others.

Large differences in the age of the artefacts makes a single deposition unlikely, and would be best accounted for by the use of this site over several centuries. The motivation for these votive offerings remains unknown. They might have been associated with everyday worship, with thanksgiving or with placating the gods in times of trouble. The latter is a strong possibility, but we have no way of knowing which deity or deities were being honoured. Were these water gods or gods of war, gods of the tribe or the place?

We do not know if any ceremonies beside the lake were enacted by Druids, although we do know that they presented a formidable appearance during the Romans' first attack on the island. The importance attached to Anglesey by Roman writers and the presence of sacred groves has always led to speculation that the island was a sacred place in itself and a major centre of Druidism at that time. The details of any rituals associated with Llyn Cerrig Bach remain unknown, and of course there is every likelihood that they changed over the centuries, as rituals do.

Cyril Fox suggested that the votive items had been thrown into the lake from an adjacent rocky platform. However the more recent study of Iron Age votive sites across Europe, and surveys of this site, have raised the possibility that Llyn Cerrig Bach included a causeway or jetty leading to a central island sanctuary, from which the watery offerings were made.

THE EVIDENCE IS CLEAR THAT LLYN CERRIG BACH WAS A RITUAL SITE WHERE PRECIOUS OBJECTS WERE LEFT AS VOTIVE OFFERINGS

A question of dates

Just when were the Llyn Cerrig Bach treasures placed in the lake?
Philip Macdonald sums up the scientific evidence

Dating the Llyn Cerrig Bach assemblage poses a significant challenge for archaeologists. The far from ideal circumstances surrounding its discovery mean that it is not possible for them to use all of the techniques they would be able to apply to a more carefully excavated group of objects.

Several distinct types of artefact are represented here. It is possible to propose broad date ranges for many of them by carefully studying the contexts of comparable discoveries in Britain and elsewhere.

When these various date ranges are compared, two broad groups of artefacts, distinct in both date and character, can be identified. The largest group consists of military equipment, vehicle fittings and harness pieces, whose vogue extends from the fourth or third centuries BC to around the middle of the first century AD. A second, smaller group, which includes the coiled mounts and the so-called casket ornaments, are all examples of non-martial types that range in date from the middle of the first century AD until at least the later second century.

This might suggest that the assemblage was the product of a single episode of deposition that occurred in the middle of the first century AD. However the earlier group contains several items, such as some of the swords and scabbard fragments, which can be confidently dated on the strength of continental parallels to the third or second century BC. This suggests that deposition occurred episodically over several centuries at Llyn Cerrig Bach.

Scientific analysis of the composition of the copper alloy artefacts from Llyn Cerrig Bach confirms the validity of this division in chronology and classification. Tiny samples taken from all the copper alloy artefacts have been analysed using a spectrometer and a scanning electron microscope. Previous studies of Iron Age and Romano-British copper alloy artefacts have indicated that arsenic is an impurity commonly present in Iron Age copper alloys, but which only rarely occurs in copper alloys of Roman date. This difference is probably a consequence of the relatively higher temperature at which smelting was undertaken during the Roman period. Analysis showed that most of the coiled mounts and all of the so-called casket ornaments, which define the later group of artefacts, were manufactured from the Romano-British alloy type, whilst nearly all of the

other copper alloy objects were of the Iron Age alloy type.

Another scientific dating method which has been successfully applied to the Llyn Cerrig Bach assemblage is radiocarbon dating. This is a technique, based upon measuring the radioactive decay of an isotope of carbon, which can be applied to most organic materials. To date, three of the animal bones from the assemblage and preserved wood associated with two pieces of ironwork have been dated. The animal bone returned date ranges of 800-200 BC, 400-180 BC and 350 BC - AD 60. The oak pole from a cart or chariot was dated between 390-200 BC and the fragment of an ash shaft preserved in the socket of one of the spearheads was dated to between 210-40 BC.

These dating techniques indicate that deposition began at Llyn Cerrig Bach by, at the latest, the end of the third century BC. It is possible that the deposition of animal bone may have begun at an earlier date than the deposition of metalwork. The analyses based upon classification and metallurgy also raise the intriguing possibility that, whilst its character may have changed, deposition continued at the site long after the Roman incursions into Anglesey.

***Dr Philip Macdonald** is Fieldwork Director with the Centre for Archaeological Fieldwork, Queen's University, Belfast*

We now know that the wood from the draught-pole is between about 2,400 and 2,200 years old

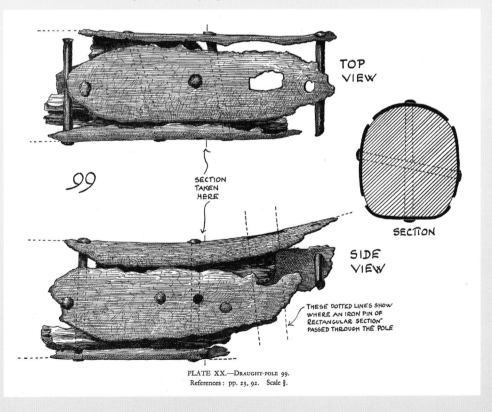

TOP VIEW

SECTION

SIDE VIEW

99

SECTION TAKEN HERE

THESE DOTTED LINES SHOW WHERE AN IRON PIN OF RECTANGULAR SECTION PASSED THROUGH THE POLE

PLATE XX.—DRAUGHT-POLE 99.
References : pp. 23, 92. Scale ⅓.

TIMELINE

LATE BRONZE AGE

- Parc-y-Meirch hoard, Conwy (harness and wagon fittings): *c.*1150–1000 BC
- Guilsfield hoard, Powys (weapons and tools): *c.*1050–950 BC

1000 BC • Early use of iron for small objects and ornaments: *c.*1000–800 BC

900 BC • Causeway and votive site: Flag Fen, Cambridgeshire: first millennium BC

EARLY IRON AGE

800 BC • Important iron working 'Hallstatt' cultures develop in Central Europe: *c.*800–400 BC
- Llyn Fawr hoard, Rhondda Cynon Taf (cauldrons, tools, Hallstatt sword): *c.*800-600 BC

600 BC • Hillforts dominate Anglesey's high ground. Occupied on and off for many centuries

500 BC • Tŷ Mawr Iron Age dwellings, Holyhead mountain. Long occupation: *c.*500 BC – AD 500
- Wooden causeway and votive offerings, Fiskerton on the River Witham, Lincolnshire: *c.*450–300 BC

MIDDLE IRON AGE

400 BC • 'Celtic' culture develops across temperate Europe: *c.*500–450 BC, at sites such as La Tène, Switzerland
- The Cerrigydrudion 'crown', Conwy county: *c.*400 BC
- Wooden bowls and sword at Breiddin hillfort, Powys: *c.*400–100 BC
- Shields, votive offerings in Rivers Witham and Thames: *c.*350–50 BC
- The Greek geographer Pythias refers to the Πρεττανοί (*Pretannoi*, Britons): *c.*330 BC
- War sanctuary, Gallic shrine at Gournay-sur-Aronde: fourth century BC
- Ironworking at Crawcwellt, near Trawsfynydd: third century BC to first century AD
- **Radiocarbon dating: three animal bones, Llyn Cerrig Bach: 800–200 BC**
- **Radiocarbon dating: oak chariot pole, Llyn Cerrig Bach: 390–200 BC**

300 BC • **Early weapon deposits at Llyn Cerrig Bach, including swords: *c.*300 BC**
- Chariot burials, Garton and Wetwang, East Yorkshire: third century BC
- **Radiocarbon dating: spear shaft fragment, Llyn Cerrig Bach: 210–40 BC**

LATE IRON AGE

200 BC • **Iron trading ('currency') bars, Llyn Cerrig Bach:** *c.* **second century BC**

• Defended settlements: Caer Lêb and Bryn Eryr, Anglesey: *c.*200 BC – AD 400

• Lead anchor stock, Porth Felen, Llŷn peninsula: second or first century BC

• Southeastern Britain: close contact with Belgic tribes from Gaul: second to first century BC

• **Bridle bits, Llyn Cerrig Bach: second to first century BC**

• **Bronze horn, Llyn Cerrig Bach: second century BC to first century AD**

100 BC • **Sickle and tongs, Llyn Cerrig Bach: second century BC to first century AD**

• **Terrets, Llyn Cerrig Bach: second century BC to first century AD**

• **Majority of swords at Llyn Cerrig Bach:** *c.***125 BC to first century AD**

• **Bronze crescentic plaque, Llyn Cerrig Bach:** *c.***100 BC**

• Bronze shield mountings, Moel Hiraddug, Dyserth: *c.*100 BC – AD 78

• The Snettisham hoard (*c.* seventy gold torcs), Norfolk: *c.*70 BC

• Romans, under Julius Caesar, invade southeastern Britain: 55–54 BC

• Julius Caesar: *De Bello Gallico* (The Gallic War): 50s–40s BC

• Engineered road, Bayston Hill, Shropshire: first century BC

• **Dagger fragment, Llyn Cerrig Bach: first century BC**

AD 1 • **Bronze shield boss mounting, Llyn Cerrig Bach: first century BC to first century AD**

• Stone ritual head, possibly of a god, Hen-dŷ, Anglesey: [date uncertain]

• Decorative iron firedog, Capel Garmon, Conwy: *c.*AD 1–100

• Burial with sword, Gelliniog Wen, Anglesey: possibly first century AD

• **Later swords at Llyn Cerrig Bach: early first century AD**

• Start of Roman conquest of Britain, under Aulus Plautius: AD 43

• Votive offerings of bronze bowls, Langstone, Newport: *c.*47–75 AD

• Tal-y-llyn shield fittings, Gwynedd: *c.*AD 50–80

• The Snowdon bowl, Gwynedd: *c.*AD 50–100

• Bronze neck collar and bracelet, Boverton, Vale of Glamorgan: *c.*AD 50–150

• 'Lindow man': ritual killing, Lindow Moss bog, Cheshire: *c.*AD 50

• **Bronze cauldron fragments, Llyn Cerrig Bach: first century AD**

• **Slave chains, Llyn Cerrig Bach: first century AD**

ROMANO-BRITISH PERIOD

• Roman invasion of Anglesey, under Suetonius Paulinus: AD 60

• Roman troops recalled from Anglesey to put down Boudicca's revolt: AD 60

• Anglesey re-invaded by the Romans under Agricola: AD 78

• Segontium Roman fort, Caernarfon: *c.*AD 78

AD 100 • Native settlement at Din Lligwy, Anglesey: *c.* first to fourth century AD

• **Bronze casket ornament and coils, Llyn Cerrig Bach: perhaps second century AD**

• Roman road and buildings, Tai Cochion, Menai Strait: *c.* first to fourth century AD

• Tacitus: *Annales* (the Annals): AD 116

AD 200 • Roman naval fort and signal station at Holyhead, Anglesey: *c.*AD 290–390

AD 300 • Christianity legalised within the Roman empire: AD 313

AD 400 • Romans withdraw from Britain: AD 401–410

FROM NEAR OR FAR?

The detective investigation now turns to questions of geography. Was this a local shrine, perhaps a deposition site for tribal booty in local raids and wars? Or did Llyn Cerrig Bach attract attention from a wider area of the British Isles?

In accordance with archaeological practice, Sir Cyril Fox compared the artefacts from Llyn Cerrig Bach with those found elsewhere – in Britain, Ireland or continental Europe. He placed them in associated groupings and classified them by type. In adopting this technique Fox estimated that the assemblage included items from Ireland and from northern, eastern, southeastern and southwestern regions of Britain. Fox considered mountainous Wales to be an area that was remote from direct La Tène cultural influence and from centres of manufacture in Iron Age Britain.

Discoveries in more recent years have shown that the real picture of production and distribution of Iron Age artefacts cannot be drawn with such clear boundaries. Styles associated with one region of Britain may overlap with those of another. We can now see that Wales was no backwater during the Iron Age, but a considerable producer of iron in its own right, and probably decorated metalwork too.

Of course the presence of many similar items at one particular location does not necessarily make that the place of manufacture. Finds may depend on cultural factors, such as varying burial customs. Artefacts may be transported, traded, or exchanged as gifts. Many of the Llyn Cerrig Bach artefacts could have been brought to Anglesey by refugees from distant fields of battle or by pilgrims prepared to travel long distances to a sacred ritual site.

There is no doubt that the Llyn Cerrig Bach assemblage does include items from various distant geographical locations in Britain and possibly Ireland. However we must also consider the fact that some items, perhaps the shield, may have been produced nearer home than was previously thought.

Any discussion about Llyn Cerrig Bach is dominated by the cataclysmic events of the year AD 60, when the Romans crossed the Menai Strait for the first time to attack and lay waste the is-land. As this date coincides with some of the votive activity at Llyn Cerrig Bach, it was inevitable that the two matters would be linked in the popular imagination. When the Roman legions were launching their assault upon tribe after tribe, did British warriors flee to the west and make increasingly desperate offerings to the gods in order to stave off defeat?

They may well have done; indeed it would be strange if there had not been some ritual or religious response to the unfolding disaster. Research into the deposition of bronze bowls in a bog at Langstone, near Newport in south Wales, suggests that this votive site was in intensive use at the time when the Romans were attacking the regional tribe, the Silures.

In their book *The Life and Death of a Druid Prince* (1989) the archaeologist Dr Anne Ross and the archaeological chemist Dr Don Robins made a highly speculative proposition, linking the votive offerings at Llyn Cerrig Bach with the Roman invasion and with the death of Lindow Man (*see* p.41), whom they suggest was himself a Druid. It is an exciting and sensationalist tale, and one that certainly cannot be proven.

We lack the evidence to prove any doomsday scenario at Llyn Cerrig Bach. Even if the Roman attack had caused panic, the waters of Llyn Cerrig Bach had already been receiving offerings for centuries beforehand – and continued to do so for some time after the conquest.

The riddles of Llyn Cerrig Bach can never be fully solved.

(opposite) This sandstone slab from Bridgeness, in Scotland, dates from about AD 142. It shows the brutal impact of the Roman conquest. The Roman attack of Anglesey must have been similarly traumatic.

THERE IS A DOOMSDAY SCENARIO ...
CAN WE RELATE THE LLYN CERRIG BACH OFFERINGS
TO THE ROMANS' DESECRATION OF ANGLESEY?

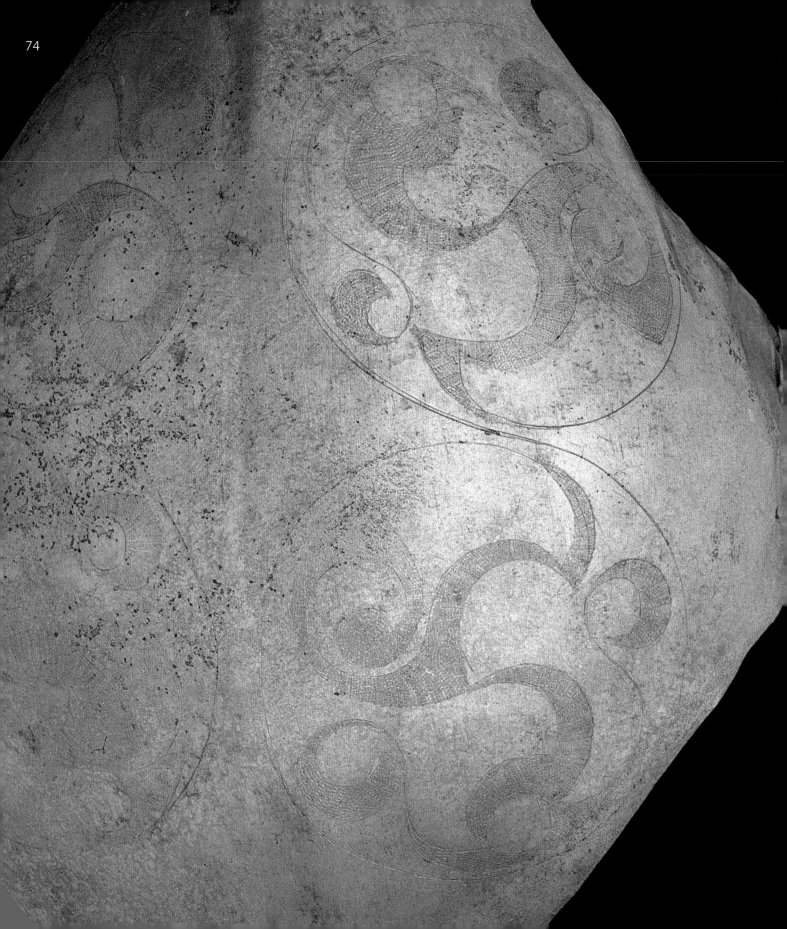

6 THE LEGACY

WHAT HAS BEEN THE AFTERMATH of the Llyn Cerrig Bach discovery? Can it still teach us useful lessons about the Iron Age?

In the 1940s the discovery of the Llyn Cerrig Bach assemblage was overshadowed by other priorities: it was wartime. The war effort could only be suspended for the briefest of windows. Information about this sensitive location was restricted for security reasons – even Sir Cyril Fox's information about the location of artefacts found near the runway could not be published at the time. By the end of the war in 1945 engineering works had completely transformed the original layout of the lake, the bog and the rock platform.

Amidst such difficulties, future exploration of the site was always going to be problematic. The airfield location of the discovery did offer one advantage, in that extensive wartime aerial photographs could be studied after the war, revealing the true extent of peat extraction. However the airfield has remained in commission ever since, so access has always been very limited and remains so.

A field survey was carried out at Llyn Cerrig Bach in 1995, led by Philip Macdonald and Tim Young. They studied the topography of the site, mapping the areas highlighted by Sir Cyril Fox with a magnetometer and a resistivity meter. Soundings were taken with an auger, identifying the area within the lake that might have been an island shrine in the Iron Age. A detailed report of the survey is included in Philip Macdonald's *Llyn Cerrig Bach* (2007).

(left) The shield boss represents the sheer splendour of Insular La Tène art and metalworking skill

The conclusion was that the peat where the artefacts had originally been located had been virtually cleared during the war, far more extensively than Cyril Fox had reported, so that chances of new items coming to light in that area were minimal. If any further material did exist, it would probably be buried under inaccessible parts of the airfield or scattered and damaged. It is quite possible that the assemblage we have is complete.

The chapter of lakeside discoveries at Llyn Cerrig Bach would seem to have closed, but the story may go on, perhaps with some chance find in the future. Other island bogs, rivers and small lakes, such as Llyn Hendref (now the bog of Cors Bodwrog) or Llyn Llywenan, Bodedern (which has a suitable lake-side platform), could have received other deposits. Archaeological investigation of other Iron Ages sites in Britain, Ireland or continental Europe may reveal further useful comparisons with items in the Llyn Cerrig Bach assemblage.

Scientific advances in metallurgy and conservation, or imaginative reconstruction work, may yet offer further insights into Iron Age craft and manufacture.

NEW DISCOVERIES AT LLYN CERRIG BACH ARE UNLIKELY. OTHER WETLAND SITES ON ANGLESEY AND IN OTHER PARTS OF WALES MAY BE WORTH FURTHER INVESTIGATION

The collection today

How is the Llyn Cerrig Bach treasure cared for, researched and made accessible?
Adam Gwilt talks about his work as curator at Amgueddfa Cymru – National Museum Wales

The material from Llyn Cerrig Bach remains an exceptional collection of international importance.

My role is to make sure that these powerful objects are properly cared for, so that present and future generations can continue to view, engage with and to wonder at them. It is equally important to be a good communicator, enabler and listener, so that this collection remains widely relevant and accessible – physically, intellectually and emotionally.

Many of the artefacts are currently displayed in our *Origins: In Search of Early Wales* archaeology galleries at National Museum Cardiff. When creating the Iron Age displays we chose to re-create the lake setting, showing the artefacts as if buried on the bottom of the lake. Further highlight objects illustrate La Tène Art, chariot equipment and ironworking technique. Each year, over 100,000 people visit this gallery, while an accompanying popular book, *Discovered in Time: Treasures from Early Wales* (2011) illustrates seventy great discoveries, including Llyn Cerrig Bach.

Those artefacts not currently displayed are carefully stored and monitored in temperature and moisture-controlled environments. The research collections are available and frequently accessed by researchers wishing to record, relate and test new ideas, often leading to new understanding. Whether we are supporting researchers preparing publications, helping pupils with school projects, or feeding the personal interests of members of the public, collections such as Llyn Cerrig Bach remain in great demand.

Amgueddfa Cymru – National Museum Wales is a centre for reporting treasure and non-treasure finds made by the public. New discoveries help us to re-interpret Llyn Cerrig Bach within its wider cultural context. Each year, the records of new finds in Wales are added to the publicly accessible Celtic Art Database for Britain and these are adding significantly to the body of Iron Age metalwork from Wales. A more complete picture is now available of those regional societies across Wales which made, displayed and buried La Tène art. As a research organisation, the National Museum engages in fieldwork and research. My own research projects – on religious and watery deposition, La Tène Art, chariots, feasting and elite display – provide relevant comparisons and insight. For example, archaeological investigation at the find-spot of a hoard of decorated bronze bowls, a wine-strainer and wooden tankard, near Langstone, Newport, has revealed that they were carefully deposited into a shallow lake during the first century AD.

Some measure of the wider appeal of Llyn Cerrig Bach is gauged through recent loans to other museums. In 2003, the decorated crescentic plaque and a chariot horse-bit were lent and shown within an ambitious temporary exhibition in Kentucky, USA, about the role of the horse in British history. The complete gang-chain was lent in 2007, to the Wilberforce House Museum in Hull, as a highlight temporary exhibit on ancient slavery, in their new galleries exploring slavery and human rights.

Although a small number of Llyn Cerrig Bach objects were lent to Oriel Ynys Môn in 2000, the 2012 exhibition included many highlight pieces which had never before returned to Anglesey for display. This was a special moment for many, including staff at the National Museum.

As the diverse contributions to this book illustrate, ideas and discoveries are constantly changing and challenging the way we re-view Llyn Cerrig Bach. Beyond doubt is its enduring capacity as a special place, to reveal new stories, generate wide interest and inspire us to think about who we once were, and who we are today.

Adam Gwilt, *left,*
is Curator of Iron Age Collections at
Amgueddfa Cymru – National Museum Wales.
Here he discusses plans for the 2012 Anglesey exhibition
with Pat West and Ian Jones of Oriel Ynys Môn

TELLING THE STORY

Public interest in Llyn Cerrig Bach is keener than ever. Archaeology in general attracts a growing following of enthusiasts of all ages and Anglesey's remarkable prehistoric, medieval and industrial sites attract visitors from all over the world.

Over the years the valuable work of organisations such as Gwynedd Archaeological Trust, Bangor University, Cadw, the Anglesey Antiquarian Society and Menter Môn have helped to foster this interest in Anglesey's past. The internet has made information about the island's sites more readily available. Evelyn Owen-Jones of Llanfaelog, the daughter of W.O. Roberts, has enthusiastically told the story of Llyn Cerrig Bach to countless school children and community groups over the years. Replicas of the artefacts allow the items to be viewed by the public as they would have originally appeared, and to be handled without risk.

The bulk of the Llyn Cerrig Bach treasure has remained in the collection of the National Museum in Cardiff since the days of Sir Cyril Fox's directorship. Amgueddfa Cymru – National Museum Wales plays a leading role in caring for, researching, presenting and interpreting the Llyn Cerrig Bach collection. Each year, it engages with large audiences across Wales and internationally, maximising access to this outstanding cultural treasure. Plans are currently underway for archaeological displays to be integrated with history collections in an ambitious redevelopment at St Fagans: National History Museum.

Anglesey's county museum, Oriel Ynys Môn, opened in 1991 and is located in Llangefni, 15 kilometres (ten miles) from Llyn Cerrig Bach. It has three items from the assemblage in its permanent collection – a spearhead, a bridle bit and a nave hoop. A few items remain in private collections.

Since 1972 Llyn Cerrig Bach itself has been marked by a commemorative plaque on the lake shore, although the site's character has changed so dramatically since 1942.

At times of quiet it is still possible to imagine an Iron Age scene, a sword wheeling through the air and sinking in the lake. Imagine its ripples spreading out to the tawny reeds.

Robert Stephenson's railway, skirting Llyn Cerrig Bach from 1848, could be regarded as the final chapter of the technological story that started in the Iron Age. His Britannia Bridge, opened in 1850, was a masterpiece of metalwork, comprising two massive rectangular tubes of wrought iron, each 461 metres in length, held together by about two million rivets. What a dream for an Iron Age smith!

Warfare is another theme which links the Llyn Cerrig Bach assemblage to the modern age. The braying horns that may have accompanied the deposition of spears, swords and chariots two thousand years ago, have today been replaced by the howling of Hawk fighter jet engines on the runways of RAF Valley.

Figuratively speaking, one might say that the ripples from those swords from Llyn Cerrig Bach are still spreading out today.

(left) Evelyn Owen-Jones introduces pupils from Ysgol y Tywyn to the lake.
(right) The Llynnon roundhouses, and *(inset)* their construction.

RECONSTRUCTED ROUNDHOUSES BY LLYNNON MILL,
LLANDDEUSANT, TAKE VISTORS BACK TO
ANGLESEY LIFE IN THE IRON AGE

Glossary

afon [*Welsh*] River.

alloy A mixture of two metals, such as bronze (copper and tin).

anneal To heat and then cool a metal in order to change its internal structure.

ard A simple plough which used a spiked pole to scratch the soil. It had no blade to turn the soil over.

arsenic A poisonous chemical element found in many minerals.

artefact An object made by humans (from the Latin 'made by skill').

assemblage A group of items that has been gathered together, or a range of objects often found together.

asymmetrical Lacking balanced proportions.

auger A tool used to bore into soil and remove samples.

bit Metal mouthpiece of a horse's bridle.

bloom A sponge-like mixture of iron and slag – an early stage of iron manufacture.

boss A knob or projection, often decorative.

braze To join together pieces of metal by heating their edges and applying a solder of metal or alloy.

bridle That part of a harness which is fitted to the horse's head.

briquetage A coarse ceramic used to hold brine (salty water) in the extraction of salt.

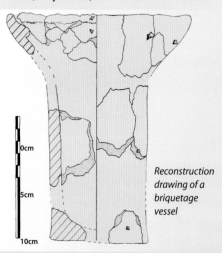

Reconstruction drawing of a briquetage vessel

bronze An alloy, typically of copper with added tin.

Bronze Age Any period characterised by the widespread use of bronze artefacts. Anglesey's Bronze Age lasted from about 2500 to 800 BC.

bryn [*Welsh*] Hill.

Brythonic That branch of the Celtic language family which later evolved into Welsh, Cornish and Breton.

cae [*Welsh*] Field.

Caergeiliog [*Welsh*] 'Fort of the cockerel'.

carnyx A long war trumpet with its mouth shaped like an animal's head.

casket ornament Decorative metalwork designed to be fixed to another object, usually a box.

cast To create an object by pouring molten metal into a mould and leaving it to cool and harden.

Celtic
[1] A branch of the Indo-European language family, including ancient languages such as Brythonic, Goidelic and Gaulish, and modern derivatives such as Welsh, Irish and Gaelic;
[2] A broad term often used to describe various cultures and artistic styles prevalent in Iron Age Europe, especially that known as La Tène;
[3] Pertaining to the kingdoms, churches and artistic styles of the far northwest of Europe in the early medieval period;
[4] Pertaining to the modern nations and territories in the far northwest of Europe.

Cerrig Bach [*Welsh*] 'Small stones' – but that is not a description of the lake shore. Llyn Cerrig Bach took its name from a small-holding to the east of the lake, known as Cerrig Bach.

chasing Engraving a metal surface with a hard metal point or chisel.

cob A building material made from clay mixed with straw.

cold-working A process of working metal by hammering.

cors [*Welsh*] Bog.

craig [*Welsh*] Rock.

Craig Carnau'r Ebolion [*Welsh*] 'Rock of the colts' hooves', named after a local farm

commote An administrative division of land in medieval Wales.

crucible A high temperature vessel in which metal is melted.

daub A render made of mud or plaster used over wattle walls.

deity A god or goddess.

deposition An item or items that have been intentionally deposited (placed) in a certain location.

desiccated Dried out, dehydrated.

die A tool or mechanical device used repeatedly to stamp, cut or shape metal.

Druid A member of the pagan priesthood in ancient Britain, Ireland and Gaul.

edge tool An implement with a cutting edge, such as a knife or chisel.

electron microscope A powerful microscope which uses electron beams to produce magnifications of up to about 10 million times.

elite A small, high-ranking group within a social order or an army.

equestrian Concerning horse-riding.

finial The ornamental end of a pole or other similar structure.

Gallic Pertaining to Gaul, an ancient region which took in parts of northern Italy, France and Belgium.

Gaulish The Celtic language spoken in ancient Gaul.

Goidelic The Celtic language spoken in ancient Ireland.

grave To incise or engrave metal or stone.

Hallstatt A Late Bronze Age and Early Iron Age culture which originated in the Danube basin, named after an archaeological site of that name in Austria.

harrow An agricultural implement that is hauled across a field to break up and level the soil.

Din Silwy hillfort, 'Bwrdd Arthur', Llanddona

hillfort Defences of stone, earth and timber enclosing an area of high ground, often with dwellings.

hoard A cache, an accumulation of objects all hidden at the same time for protection or future use.

horn cap A cap to a horn tip (as found at Llyn Cerrig Bach) now thought to decorate the upturned ends of a chariot yoke.

horse collar Part of a harness, a padded ring placed around a horse's neck and shoulders to help it haul a cart or a plough.

imperial Of an empire.

Indo-European A major group of related languages, which includes most European languages and many Asian ones.

ingot A block or bar of metal ready for casting.

insular
[1] Relating to islands;
[2] Relating to art styles influenced by La Tène which manifested themselves in Britain and Ireland in the late Iron Age.

Iron Age Any period characterised by the widespread use of iron artefacts. Anglesey's Iron Age is generally dated from about 800 BC until the Roman conquest.

La Tène An influential Iron Age culture named after an archaeological site of that name in Switzerland.

libation The pouring of a liquid, such as a wine or a potion, as an offering to a deity.

Llanfair yn Neubwll [*Welsh*] 'Saint Mary's of the Two Pools'.

Llanfihangel yn Nhowyn (Nhywyn) [*Welsh*] 'Saint Michael's in the Dunes'.

llyn [*Welsh*] Lake.

lost wax process A method of making a mould for casting metals. Moist clay was packed around a wax model. When the clay was baked, the wax melted, leaving a vacant space which could be filled with molten metal.

linch-pin A peg securing a wheel to an axle.

magnetometer An instrument used to measure magnetism of the earth, which can map buried objects and structures.

Trwyn y Parc promontory fort, Bodorgan

malleable Of metals, capable of being shaped by hammering.

marram A stiff grass which grows along coasts, stabilising sand dunes.

martial Related to warfare.

megalithic Using very large stones, as in the burial chambers of the Neolithic period.

meteoric iron Iron obtained from meteorites, a source for the earliest users of iron.

metallurgy The science and practice of metalworking.

midden An ancient refuse heap.

molten Liquefied by heat.

mortar A stone bowl designed for the grinding of foodstuffs or other materials, using a hand-held rod called a pestle.

motif An element of pattern within a design.

mould-board The board or blade of a plough which turns over the soil to make a furrow.

nave The wooden hub of a cartwheel or chariot wheel.

nave-hoop A metal band used to prevent a nave splitting.

oxidation The chemical interaction of a substance with oxygen, as in the rusting of iron.

pagan Non-Christian religious beliefs, such as those of Iron Age Europe.

peat Undecomposed vegetable matter, forming the rich black soil found in bogs and marshes.

pelta-shaped A double-crescent shape, named after an ancient shield type.

polymath A learned person who knows about many different subjects.

promontory fort A hillfort built on a headland, using cliffs as part of its defences.

quench To cool suddenly, by plunging in water.

radiocarbon dating Finding the age of organic materials by measuring their radioactive carbon content.

raising Working a convex sheet of metal by hammering the outer surface.

Rhosneigr [*Welsh*] 'The heath belonging to Neigr' (a noble who fought against Irish invaders in *c*.AD 450).

repoussé Metal raised in relief by hammering from the rear side.

resistivity meter Any instrument designed to measure underground electrical resistance, often used in archaeological survey.

Romano-British The culture of Roman-occupied Britain AD 43–*c*.410

roundhouse A circular dwelling common in Iron Age Britain.

scabbard The sheath or cover for a sword.

sinking Working a convex sheet of metal by hammering from the inside.

slag Vitreous matter separated from the metal during the smelting of ore.

slag inclusion analysis: the chemical analysis of microscopic slag inclusions in iron in order to determine the origin of the iron.

smelt To fuse or melt ore in order to extract its metal content.

spectrometer An instrument which analyses the structure of objects by measuring wavelength, energy, intensity, etc.

steel A hard, tough form of iron, treated to have a carbon content of between 0.2% (mild steel) and 1.7% (high carbon steel).

swastika Any design in which the arms of a cross are bent at right angles.

tang A protruding tongue of metal used to fix a blade to its handle.

tempering To treat metal by heating and cooling in order to control its qualities.

tenon A projecting tongue fitting into a socket: as in the 'mortise and tenon joint' used in woodwork or masonry.

terret Rings which hold a horse's reins and prevent them from tangling.

torc An ornamental neck ring often made from twisted strands of metal.

triskele A design motif in which three elongated shapes radiate from a centre (from the Greek for 'three-legged').

triumph A victory parade in ancient Rome.

tywyn [*Welsh*] Sand dune(s).

votive offering An offering made to a deity, accompanied by a vow or dedication.

war sanctuary A temple or shrine dedicated to a war deity, and housing armour and weapons captured in battle.

wattle Walls or fences made of interwoven wooden staves.

weld To fuse together two sections of metal by a process of heating and hammering.

withers The highest point on a horse's back.

wrought iron A malleable form of iron which has never been liquid. It is tough and yet easy to work by hammering, contrasting with cast iron which is brittle.

ynys [*Welsh*] Island.

yoke A wooden bar across the shoulders, joining together two draught animals, such as oxen or horses.

Further information

BOOKS

Frances Lynch, *Prehistoric Anglesey*,
Anglesey Antiquarian Society 1991

Philip Macdonald, *Llyn Cerrig Bach: A Study of the
Copper Alloy Artefacts from the Insular La Tène
Assemblage*, University of Wales Press 2007

Philip Steele & Robert Williams, *Môn Mam Cymru:
the Guide to Anglesey*, Llyfrau Magma 2006
www.llyfrau–magma.co.uk

Mick Sharp, Jean Williamson & Frances Lynch,
Anglesey: Past landscapes of the coast,
Windgather Press 2009

Places to visit

ANGLESEY

Llyn Cerrig Bach (OS114 SH306765), by Valley airfield.
*The most important British example of an Iron Age
sacred lake.*

Din Lligwy Iron Age settlement (OS114 SH497861),
near Moelfre. *A Romano-British group of houses and
working buildings arranged within a wall.*

Din Silwy hillfort, 'Bwrdd Arthur' (OS114 SH586814),
Llanddona. *A flat-topped hill surrounded by a broad
stone wall.*

Llynnon roundhouses (OS114 SH341853), by Llynnon
windmill, Llanddeusant. (Seasonal opening).
Impressively reconstructed roundhouses.

Caer y Twr (OS114 SH218830), Holyhead Mountain.
Later prehistoric hillfort and Roman signal station.

Tŷ Mawr huts (OS114 SH212820), Holyhead Mountain.
*The remains of 10 large stone huts of the Iron Age,
interspersed with smaller rectangular buildings.*

FURTHER AFIELD

Tre'r Ceiri hillfort (OS123 SH373446), Llanaelhaern.
The most spectacular Iron Age hillfort in north Wales.

Castell Caer Lleion (OS115 SH760778), Conwy
Mountain. *A well defended hillfort with the remains of
about 50 stone huts.*

Segontium Roman auxiliary fort (OS115 SH485624),
Caernarfon. *The main Roman base in north Wales
from the conquest to the end of the fourth century.*

MUSEUM COLLECTIONS

Oriel Ynys Môn, Llangefni, Anglesey.

Gwynedd Museum, Bangor.

National Museum Cardiff.

The British Museum, London.

The National Museum of Ireland, Dublin.

Laténium, Neuchâtel, Switzerland.

Picture credits

© **The National Museum of Wales**
Photographs of the Llyn Cerrig Bach artefacts on the
front cover and pages 9, 16, 17, 18, 34, 36 (Cerrigydrudion crown), 51, 54, 55, 56, 57, 59, 60, 61, 62, 65, 66, 69, 74.
Photographs on pages 11 & 57 (chained captives), 13,
16, 17, 77.
Line drawings by C.O. Waterhouse on pages 12, 14, 15,
24, 48, 55, 57, 59, 69; by Cyril Fox 52; by Tony Daly 60
(decoration on short tongs).

**Copyrights are also retained by the following
institutions and individuals, with all rights reserved**

Menter Môn (with funding from the Heritage Lottery
Fund, Cadw and Welsh Assembly Government) /
illustrations by Brian Byron: 27, 35, 45, 27, 61 (smithy),
64 (roundhouse interior).

Gwynedd Archaeological Trust: 81 (magnetometer), 82.

Gwynedd Archaeological Trust /
David Longley: 81 (Din Silwy).

Ian Jones, Capel Coch: 4, 75.

Ancient Music Ireland: Loughnashade and Ard Brinn
horns, 58/59, www.ancientmusicireland.com. (The
reproduction horns were made by John Creed.)

Osprey Publishing / illustration by Angus McBride: 53.

Paul Birkbeck / English Heritage Images: 33.

English Heritage / illustration by Ivan Lapper: 43.

Tim Young / GeoArch: 20, 21, www.GeoArch.co.uk.

National Museums Scotland / www.scran.ac.uk: 73.

Elaine Morris (after W.J. Britnell): 80

The Fitzwilliam Museum: 53

Latenium, Neuchâtel / Jacques Roethlisberger: 19

Gwyn Williams, Llansadwrn: 70.

Anglesey County Archives: 8 (railway plan).

Ancient Arts: 79 (inset pictures).

Llyfrau Magma: 12 (book), 32, 38 (Hen-dŷ head), 39, 41
(lake margin), 46/47, 68, 75, 78, 79 (main picture).

Oriel Ynys Môn: 11 (gang chain), 71 & back cover (spear on
loan to the Oriel by Menna Lloyd Williams, Aberystwyth).

British Museum Images / Trustees of the British Museum:
30, 37 (Snettisham torc), 41 ('Lindow man'), 36
(Aylesford bucket & Desborough mirror).

Peter Crew, Penrhyndeudraeth: 50 (Garton Slack), 63.

Newgrange Visitor Centre: 48 (stone spirals).

Evelyn Owen-Jones, Llanfaelog: 10, 11 (letter).

Warlord Games / illustration by Peter Dennis, 31.
(Front cover artwork from *Hail Caesar Army Lists – Biblical
to classical* © Warlord Games Ltd 2012. All rights
reserved. www.warlordgames.com).

akg-images / illustrations by Peter Connolly:
28 & 55 (Iron Age couple), 50 (burial).

Steve Greaves, Barnsley: 44 (re-enactment by the 'Ermine
Street Guard'), www.stevegreaves.com

Werner Forman Archive/ National Museum, Copenhagen /
Heritage-Images: 37, 38, 64 (Gundestrup cauldron).

Landesmuseum, Mainz: 56 (Roman carving).

Collection of the Countryside Council for Wales: 6.

Acknowledgements

**Llyfrau Magma and Oriel Ynys Môn are
grateful to the following for their assistance
during the preparation of this book**

Ann Benwell

Siôn Caffell

Peter Dennis

Sally Ellis

Steve Greaves

Alun Gruffydd

Neil Johnstone

Ian Jones

Simon & Maria O'Dwyer

Maldwyn Peris

Richard Price

John Ratcliffe

Tomos Roberts

Charles Scott-Fox

John Smith

Gwyn Williams

Menna Lloyd Williams

Staff of Amgueddfa Cymru

Anglesey County Archives, Llangefni

Menter Môn, Llangefni

Gwynedd Archaeological Trust

Countryside Council for Wales, Bangor

Ancient Arts, Degannwy

Ysgol y Tywyn, Llanfihangel yn Nhowyn

CYNGOR SIR
YNYS MÔN
ISLE OF ANGLESEY
COUNTY COUNCIL

Oriel Ynys Môn, Llangefni LL77 7TQ
℡ 01248 724444

Index

Numbers in italics represent illustrations